The Messiah Method

The Seven Disciplines of the Winningest College Soccer Program in America

Michael Zigarelli

The Messiah Method
The Seven Disciplines of the Winningest College Soccer Program in America
by Michael Zigarelli

Printed in the United States of America

ISBN 9781613790250

Cover photo by Sarah DiPaola

www.xulonpress.com

Dedication

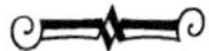

For all the coaches and players of the
Messiah College soccer program who have shown us
that there is a higher purpose than winning,
that team comes before individual, and
that excellence can be a way of life.

Table of Contents

Preface and Acknowledgements

Many outsiders have tried to explain why the Messiah College soccer teams win so many games, among them CBS Sports, *USA Today*, *The New York Times* and an array of local newspapers and bloggers. I'm delighted that they have. This is a story worth telling.

I admit, though, to being not entirely satisfied with their explanations. They tend to do a fine job of describing the "what" but not the "how"—the results but not the means by which this program gets results. Much of the time, that "how" piece, the critical piece for any leader who wants to replicate Messiah's success, is a bit over-simplified, with important elements downplayed or missing altogether.

I don't intend that to be a criticism. That's just life in a sound-bite world. But by contrast, this is not a sound-bite book. It's a more in-depth look at this college soccer program, both the men's team and the women's team, a program whose combined winning percentage from 2000 to 2010 was the highest in the country for Division I, II, or III.

It's a book about the "how," in particular, how excellence happens.

A few caveats, though. Truth in advertising. First, this is not an insider account. I never played soccer for Messiah.

I never coached there. I never even attended Messiah. So, like those news agencies, I too am essentially an outsider. However, as a Messiah College faculty member, I've had special access to the people and the soccer archives necessary to perform the research—dozens of interviews, copious secondary materials, a wealth of vital "insider" information.

Second, this is not a biography. Those who are looking for a history of the Messiah soccer program will no doubt be disappointed with this resource. I am not an historian; my fields are leadership and strategy. Perhaps predictably, then, this is a book about leadership and strategy. My basic research question has been *how do they do it?* What's the process these teams have followed to achieve excellence and to sustain it year after year? And how can we do the same with our own teams, in and out of sports?

Third, I've worked hard to take a dispassionate look at my subject, but still, my conclusions may not be entirely objective. This has been the easiest and hardest book project on which I've ever worked. "Easiest" because I love the sport and this soccer program, and it's been an absolute joy to learn what it's really all about. "Hardest" because as a researcher, one needs to maintain impartiality. As you'll see for yourself, though, it's sometimes difficult not to be impressed by these people and this organization. Frankly, I'm a bit relieved that the writing is complete and I can now go back to being a fan.

All that to say: *The Messiah Method* is surely not a perfect resource, but I've crafted it with as much care and integrity as I can muster. So many people have invested so very much to make the Messiah soccer program extraordinary. My goal has been to work just as hard to accurately convey both the "what" and "how" of their success. My hope, and indeed my prayer, is that this book will honor them and at the same time, that it will be helpful to you, no matter what kind of team you lead.

A special thanks to the Messiah College head coaches who generously shared their time and perspective to make this book possible—Dave Brandt, Scott Frey, Brad McCarty, and Layton Shoemaker. I'm also deeply indebted to the legion of other interviewees and contributors who effervesced with insights and stories about this unique soccer program: Todd Balsbaugh, Jake Berry, Nick Blossey, Greg Clippinger, Jared Clugston, Terry Earhart, Aaron Faro, Drew Frey, Kyle Fulks, Barry Goodling, Dan Haines, Susan Hasseler, Erin Hench, Randy Herndon, Katie Hoffsmith, Amy Horst, Tim Houseal, Kelsey Gorman, Kacie Klynstra, Hannah (Levesque) Leatherman, Savannah (Stolzenburg) Lehman, Mike Miller, Sheldon Myer, Jennifer Myhre, Trey Overholt, Rob Pepper, Geoff Pezon, Kent Ramirez, Mike Russ, Mindy (Miller) Smith, Jason Spodnik, Todd Suessmuth, Bethany (Swanger) Sauer, Troy Sauer, Aaron Schwartz, Dustin Shambach, Leah Sipe, Nick Thompson, Josh Wood, Marcus Wood, Sam Woodworth, and Corinne Wulf.

I thank you all for graciously allowing this outsider to report the inside scoop on *The Messiah Method*.

Michael Zigarelli
August 2011

The Messiah Method
How Excellence Happens

From 2000 to 2010, the Messiah College soccer program—that is, the men's team and women's team combined—was the winningest NCAA soccer program in America. In fact, few others even came close. Messiah's regular and post-season record during this time was 472 wins, 31 losses, and 20 ties, for a winning percentage of .922. By comparison, the second winningest college soccer program, Trinity University in Texas, had a combined men's and women's winning percentage of .884, and the extraordinary teams at the University of North Carolina, the top Division I program during this time period, posted a winning percentage of .816.

Other stats may be even more impressive. No soccer program at any level has claimed the men's and women's NCAA national title in the same year—except for Messiah. They've done that three times (nearly five times, actually, since in two seasons the men's team finished first and the women second). Also, since 2000, the women have lost a miserly 13 games and none at home since 2006. The team amassed a 76-game unbeaten streak, they've been to eight of the last nine Final Fours, they were three times the national runner-up, and they've hoisted the Division III (D3) NCAA trophy three times.

On the men's side, where there tends to be even more parity than in D3 women's soccer, Messiah has claimed eight of the last eleven national titles, posting a perfect 8-0 record in championship games. Lots of close calls, but when they've gotten there, they've won. Consider this counter-intuitive stat as well: Since 2000, the men's post-season record is 42-3, surpassing even their regular season winning percentage—astonishing, since the caliber of competition jumps dramatically in November.

Well, obvious question: How does Messiah College do it? What's the secret of success? And, more broadly, what can we learn, whether we're leading a sports team or a business or a school or a church or any other organization, about how to achieve high performance and sustain it year after year?

That's what this book is about, their method for success, *The Messiah Method*. Cumulatively over decades, the coaching staffs have painstakingly refined a process for chronic excellence that is, in fact, transferrable to just about any team. But before we overview that Method, let's first meet the architects of it.

The Makers of the Method

Dave Brandt

Men's Coach 1997-2008, Assistant Men's Coach 1988-1996, Messiah Player 1981-1984

His former players describe him with Millennial Generation terms like "crazy soccer genius" and "freakishly good coach." Parents have written accolades like: "We were lucky enough to send you our three sons and you sent us back three fine young men." And his former coach, Layton Shoemaker, describes him as "uniquely intense," a characteristic that he says dates back decades to Brandt's playing days.

Dave Brandt the player has career stats that rank him among Messiah's best: 35 assists and 55 goals, including 18 game-winners. But Dave Brandt the coach has no peer at any college. When he left Messiah after the 2008 season to take the head coaching position at the US Naval Academy, he simply had the best record of any NCAA men's soccer coach in history: 247 wins, 25 losses, 14 ties. In four of the twelve years he led the Messiah men's team, he was honored as the National Soccer Coaches Association of America D3 Coach of the Year.

Importantly, Brandt departed Messiah with more than a legacy of wins and championships. He also left a legacy of transformed lives. Here's just a sampling of commendations from former players, shared on a tribute blog after he resigned:

- "You have been the single-most influential person in my life…I am a better person because of you and your program."
- "There is no way that I'll ever forget you or the impact you had on my life as a young man who had no idea how to navigate his life."
- "Thank you with everything that is in me for changing my life, for impacting me for eternity."
- "I have more respect for Coach Brandt than any man I've ever known…He has taught me about doing the right thing for its own sake."

As more than one alumnus told me, Coach Brandt would say: "The longer you are in this program, the more you'll understand it's really not about soccer." Brandt confirmed that in our interview, adding: "We're using soccer as a vehicle and it's affecting lives, without a doubt."

The longer you are in this program,
the more you'll understand
it's really not about soccer.

Dave Brandt
Men's Coach, 1997-2008

Scott Frey
Women's Coach 2000-present, Assistant Men's Coach 1988-1992, Messiah Player 1980-1984

"Scott's the best in the business." The comment came from rival head coach, Marcus Wood, after his team narrowly edged Messiah in the 2010 National Championship. For years Wood had been picking Scott's brain, benchmarking Messiah, learning all he could about how to transform his Hardin-Simmons University program. And that day the student excelled the teacher, but then spoke for countless other "students" at that post-game press conference: "They're a model and we're trying to replicate a lot of the things they're doing."

Frey (pronounced "fry") enjoyed a solid career as a Messiah player, his years overlapping Brandt's. As an alumnus, Frey returned to Messiah to assist with the men's team before taking the helm at Alma College in Michigan, ultimately winning a couple conference titles and advancing to the Men's Final Four in 1999. The next year, Frey returned to Messiah to lead the women's program. Through 2010, he compiled a record of 229 wins, 13 losses and 11 ties, officially earning the D3 Women's Soccer Coach of the Year honors in 2005 and 2009 and, apparently, unofficially earning the honor from at least one admirer as "the best in the business." (In fact, he's pretty close in the women's game—second only to legendary UNC coach Anson Dorrance in winning percentage.)

Like Brandt, Frey guides his team to win not just soccer games, but to win at life as well. Legions of current and former players attest to his kindhearted mentorship. His last lines of a recent email to the girls offer but one telling snapshot: "Have a great day. Make the most of it. Tell someone you love them. Your parents would really appreciate it, I promise."

For Scott Frey, too, this job is about so much more than soccer.

Layton Shoemaker
Men's Coach 1974-1996

"Layton is the grandfather of the program." So says a resolute Dave Brandt. "And he was a second father figure to me and many others. His influence on my life and on how I think was significant."

Shoemaker came to Messiah after coaching for seven years at Barrington College in Rhode Island. In his 23 years as the Messiah men's coach, he led the program to national titles in the National Christian College Athletic Association (NCCAA) in 1978 and 1981, he was the D3 Men's Soccer Coach of the Year in 1986, and he tallied a career record of 316 wins, 96 losses and 27 ties.

Along the way, he learned a number of coaching strategies and philosophies from the faithful study of what John Wooden had done at UCLA (which arguably, then, makes Wooden the "great-grandfather" of the Messiah program!)"It didn't matter that he was a basketball coach," says Shoemaker. "He could have been a cricket coach. But Wooden had to be doing something right."

Shoemaker was also a bit of a Renaissance man, serving simultaneously as soccer coach, Athletic Director for 15 years, Chair of the Health, Physical Education and Recreation Department for 17 years, and teaching courses almost every semester. His work ethic was fabled and through it, he laid the foundation for the stunning success of the program after he left, though that's not always recognized. Messiah sweeper and long-time program supporter Dan Haines put it well: "The foundation on a house is ultimately the part you don't see ... From where we all sit today, it may be a little harder to see what Layton did. But it's definitely there, underneath it all."

Brad McCarty

Men's Coach 2009-present, Assistant Men's Coach 2001-2008, Messiah Player 1989-1992

Haines continued: "If Layton laid the foundation and Dave built the house, then Brad is building an addition onto the house—and it's a *significant* addition."

Indeed it is. For starters, it's an addition of two national championships in his first two years in charge, making Brad McCarty the only NCAA soccer coach to pull that off. He did so, in part, because he has the humility not to fix what's not broken, and at the same time, the wisdom to adapt Messiah's approach to a competition that has been incessantly studying his team for years.

Back in the day, McCarty was a talented Messiah player who then went on to play pro for four years, later coaching college teams in Kansas and South Carolina before returning to Messiah as the Assistant Men's Coach. He's led the men's team since spring 2009, a year when he continued the tradition of his predecessors by earning the D3 Men's Soccer Coach of the Year award.

If Layton laid the foundation and Dave built the house, then Brad is building an addition onto the house—and it's a significant addition.

Dan Haines
Class of 1983

A father of four, McCarty's posture is more than that of a firm disciplinarian. It's also one of a benevolent and sometimes lighthearted shepherd. He recognizes that though these athletes are national champs, warriors on the field and legends in the trophy case, they're still kids and he handles them as such. Case in point: While I was interviewing McCarty in his office, a player brought in a personal check for some equipment. McCarty handed it back saying it wasn't signed, after which the kid signed his check—in the memo line. Gently, with only the slightest smirk, McCarty edified him that we sign checks on the bottom right.

The program is clearly in good hands with their new coach. According to Brandt, "Brad has a full and complete understanding of the critical elements (of the system) on and off the field." And he can clearly execute that understanding, conceding a mere two losses in his first two years with the reigns. Like Brandt and Frey, he uses The Messiah Method to get results. Let's look now at what that Method entails.

The Messiah Method

Their pace of play is rapid, the technical proficiency superb. Their first touch—often *the* distinguishing skill separating the best teams from all the others—is predictably tight. Ball speed and passing accuracy are impressive, honed through untold hours of passing drills. They find each other's feet well.

The defense is swift and swarming, the goalkeeping is sound and often heroic. Tirelessly, these fittest of teams run others ragged by spreading opponents across the full 80 yard width of their home pitch and by constantly crashing the attacking third to gain a numerical advantage. In the midfield, they usually know where their teammates will be without even looking up. On a crisp Pennsylvania night, their on-the-field communication is heard halfway across campus.

If a team manages to take Messiah to overtime, they better have another gear available. Since 2000, the women have lost only four of 25 overtime games, winning 16 times; the men's OT record even exceeds that, losing only four of 39, and winning 26.

These are athletes with the knowledge, skill and poise to play at any D3 school or, for that matter, at many D2 or D1 schools. Perhaps more importantly, they operate as a unit, with a flow and a rhythm that is beautiful, in the soccer sense of the word, and often masterful.

But this beauty is simply an outcome, just as the win-loss record and championship trophies are an outcome. They're all the result of something else—something that teams who are just as fit and just as fast and just as talented and just as determined to win cannot yet seem to replicate. As Assistant Women's Coach Todd Balsbaugh revealed: "The winning isn't what happens on the field. Ninety-five percent of it is what happens before we ever get to the field."

That's the primary research question of this project: What does that 95 percent entail? What's the process that enables the unprecedented, breakthrough success these teams have enjoyed? What's "The Messiah Method"?

In short, it's a series of habits or disciplines, seven in particular. And the good news is that every leader can glean from it, maybe even import the Method wholesale into his or her environment. It's a reproducible model for those who have the patience and courage to adopt it, no matter what kind of team they lead.

Some of these habits may be an epiphany, others may seem yawningly obvious, but in operation each is a challenge. To orchestrate any one of them with consistency requires effort and expertise; to orchestrate all of them requires a master conductor.

It's possible, though, as these coaches have demonstrated, and it's possible in or out of sports. Here's an overview of the seven disciplines that have generated such extraordinary results at Messiah College.

Pursue a Higher Purpose Than Winning

"I'll never forget something that Coach Frey said during my sophomore year," reflected 2003 All-American Erin (Benedict) Bills in a note to her former team. "A teammate had graduated and said she missed the summer workouts... I thought, 'yeah, right, like I'll ever look back and miss those!' Coach said something to the effect of 'the only thing worse than running is not having something to run for.'"

For generations, Messiah players have indeed had "something to run for"—something more than themselves or their reputation, something more than winning, and even something more than championships. In fact, almost everyone associated with both the men's and women's programs is quick to point out that winning is decidedly *not* the goal at Messiah.

Of course, neither is losing. These players are exceedingly competitive and badly want to win. But it's not their purpose. Instead, they remain focused on "playing for the name on the front of their jerseys," a higher purpose that prioritizes sportsmanship and character development and "team over individual." More than that, this perspective may actually influence their on-the-field results because it supercharges their work ethic, it encourages smarter, more selfless play, and it builds team unity—the elusive competitive advantage of striving toward a common goal.

It's unorthodox in athletics, but each day the Messiah teams "pursue a higher purpose than winning." It's the cornerstone discipline for them, the one that aligns and buttresses all the others.

The only thing worse than running
is not having something to run for.

Scott Frey
Women's Coach

Be Intentional About Everything

Expert leadership is not separated out as one of the seven disciplines in this book because, frankly, it's integrated throughout each of them. It is, in a sense, what this book is about from cover to cover—talented coaches who have created a success model and executed it with excellence.

Where these coaches may distinguish themselves the most, perhaps, is by being *intentional about everything*, by insisting on getting things right no matter how small, by attending to—even obsessing over—detail. From communicating the purpose, to designing the world's best recruiting visit, to proactively managing team chemistry, to consistently confronting mediocrity, to developing the passing patterns that will take them from the centerback to the back of the net, as Coach Frey says: "there's not much we don't orchestrate."

This is a leadership philosophy that traces its Messiah roots to Dave Brandt and his core assumption: "If you don't like what's happening on your team, it's your fault." It's the kind of revelation that can change everything for a coach or almost any other leader. The truth is you have all the power you need. You can make your team and your program what you want it to be … provided you put in the work.

How essential is this discipline? How much has it really mattered at Messiah? Brandt's bottom line is this: "Intentionality may be the biggest part of our success."

Recruit "Both-And" Players

The Messiah Method rejects the assumption that we must choose between players of the highest caliber and players of the highest character—between talented athletes and selfless, team players. For Messiah this has long been a "both-and" proposition, not an "either-or." There's no tradeoff and no room for compromise.

It wasn't always that way, explains Brandt. "What happened with men's soccer (in the late 1990s) is we redefined what success was. Messiah athletes had always emphasized the Christian aspect. What was lost a little was the ability to compete, to be a little bit tough. We didn't want one or the other. We wanted both."

So Brandt raised the bar on recruiting, an approach that Scott Frey also implemented soon after his arrival in 2000. And over time, the coaches devised increasingly-effective ways to identify and sign these elusive "both-and" prospects—primarily Christian kids who were being recruited at the D1 and D2 levels.

Brandt sums up the philosophy by admiringly quoting Herb Brooks, the gold medal hockey coach who transformed the 1980 US Olympic squad: "I'm not looking for the best players. I'm looking for the right players."

Cultivate Team Chemistry

"Team chemistry," a commonplace term in sports, refers to how well players get along with one another, how much they care for one another, and how well they can anticipate each other's moves and synergize their efforts.

At Messiah, though, "team chemistry isn't something that we just hope for," says Coach McCarty. "It's something that we work really hard at. It's not easy, it's not simple, and it doesn't just happen." Rather, Messiah has designed specific processes to build and protect relationships. "There are so many little things that have happened along the way that have created this culture," says Frey about the women's team. "You've gotta keep pushing. You've gotta keep it going."

For the coach who's willing to invest the time, there's a generous payoff, including maximum effort year-round, top recruits who are attracted to the rare and refreshing environment, and a team that consistently pulls together in must-win situations. In fact, team chemistry is at the center of the seven disciplines in this book because it's become the center of Messiah's competitive advantage.

Link All Training to the Match

"It's a fluid game with lots of moving parts." McCarty grimaces, shaking his head at the challenge. "You've got 11 out there and there are no time outs. It's not like American football where you've got plays, or like basketball where there are only five guys and lots of stoppages and it's so much smaller."

Soccer is an unstructured and sometimes chaotic sport. But the most effective teams bring order to that chaos, designing a system of play that can efficiently and predictably create dangerous opportunities. At Messiah, it begins with the leaders' crystal clear vision of what the game should look like and of the options that each player has in almost every situation. It's a high understanding of the game, for sure, though once a coach finally gains this vision, he or she can train to it.

But how exactly does that vision go from the coach's head to the players' heads—and feet—and ultimately become a reality on the field? From specific, imported drills to incessant teaching to doing everything at game intensity to innovative training for mental toughness, Messiah has found a way.

Every coach knows this, many fewer accomplish it: Training should be closely linked to the match. As we'll see, it's an advantage Messiah enjoys, one that even the teams they've played in Brazil can't seem to replicate.

Choreograph Game Day

Purpose and preparation are not enough. Capability and chemistry are not enough. To win, a team needs to execute.

Execution requires readiness and readiness is no accident. At Messiah, it happens by design, through road-tested, time-honored processes—both home and away, both before and during the match—that culminate in peak performance.

In short, they choreograph game day. For home games, that means routines and traditions to keep players focused and to connect them back to those alumni who came before them. For overnight trips, that means conceiving shared, team-building experiences that unify and keep them mentally-prepared. In either venue, for the coaches it means investing in powerful habits that make them more effective leaders.

Overall, the choreography creates an environment that enables players to thrive. And as usual, intentionality and attention to detail are touchstones of success.

The winning isn't what happens on the field. Ninety-five percent of it is what happens before we ever get to the field.

Todd Balsbaugh
Class of 1994, Assistant Women's Coach

Play to a Standard

After both Messiah teams again claimed the D3 national championship in 2009, a reporter joked with Coach Frey at the post-game press conference, asking: Instead of playing the Final Four, "should the NCAA just start mailing the trophies to Messiah every year?"

Frey managed only a slight grin, replying: "That's the perception, but it's never that easy. These two programs work unbelievably hard all the time. There's never any down time. Our players are just so motivated."

On the men's side that weekend, Danny Thompson, who may have the distinction of being the only player at Messiah (or maybe anywhere else) who was carefree enough to eat a sandwich while being interviewed at a post-game press conference, explained between bites just how hard it is to sustain this level of success: "I think it gets more difficult year after year to repeat … It's easy to fall into complacency, a false sense of security … But we can't expect the same result. We have to go out and earn it. We have to battle that false sense of security … by being the aggressor on the field and going at teams … It's a huge challenge every year."

In a sport where so many teams win it all just once in a generation, how does Messiah repeat—repeatedly?

Both the men's and the women's team have met that challenge through what they call "playing to a standard." Coach Brandt elaborates: "Playing to a standard is a higher calling than winning. The problem with making winning the highest calling is this: After you win, the question becomes *where do we go from here?*" Messiah avoids that problem, he continues, by making excellence—even perfection—their standard. So there's always somewhere else to go, a higher level to attain, something even more exciting to accomplish. It's now woven its way into the DNA of their program, but the tendencies that keep them on top are transferrable to every team.

This Doesn't Happen Overnight

Collectively, these seven disciplines, as well as some other habits that we'll consider in the last chapter, comprise Messiah's success model, a transcendent method that they've increasingly refined during the past fifteen years or so. But as almost every one of these players and coaches will tell you, *they stand on the shoulders of those who came before them*, those who laid the groundwork for the unprecedented success the program now enjoys.

It's an important reminder for any change-minded leader. The road to the top is long and circuitous.

In fact, the women's program, which launched in 1988, took 18 years to win an NCAA title. The men's program kicked-off in 1967 and took 34 years to win an NCAA title. At Messiah, championship results have required years of dedicated work, actually decades.

During those decades, Messiah fielded plenty of talented teams. Before Scott Frey took over, the Messiah women posted a respectable 117-74-9 record, though they never quite made it to the NCAA post-season. The Messiah men have more of a storied history, boasting a winning percentage of .751 during Layton Shoemaker's 23-season tenure. In addition to their NCCAA titles in 1978 and 1981, and a runner-up year in 1980, they joined the NCAA in the early 80s, earning Final Four berths in 1986 and 1988. Their '88 semi-final battle with UC San Diego was nothing short of epic, with a crescendo of 13 rounds of penalty kicks before Messiah gave way. (By the way, UCSD went on to handily win the final that year 3-0, suggesting, albeit painfully, that Messiah may have been but a PK away from their first NCAA title back then.)

In all, before the Dave Brandt era, the men made the NCAA playoffs in half of the years in which they were eligible. Then, breakthrough. They've been invited to every post-season since, making deep runs in most of them. So have the women playing for Scott Frey.

The lesson for leaders: Be patient. "It took years and years," says Frey. "This just didn't happen overnight. It's been an ongoing process." That lesson is true of the modern program as well. Brandt didn't claim a national title until his fourth season of reshaping the program; Frey not until his sixth season with the new paradigm.

So, memo to coaches and all other team leaders: The method described in this book works, but it will require time and tenacity. Tell your team. Tell your boss. Then, tell your mirror. That person may need more convincing than any of the others.

It's a long but exhilarating journey, but it's how excellence happens. We turn next to step one.

Appendix

Final Records, Messiah College Men's Team and Women's Team

Men's Team, Year-by-Year Results

Year	Coach	W	L	T	Postseason
1967	Drescher	1	8	0	
1968	Drescher	1	9	1	
1969	Barr	1	10	0	
1970	Barr	5	6	0	
1971	Sweimler	7	7	0	
1972	Sweimler	13	5	1	NCCA and NAIA Playoffs
1973	Robertson	8	5	3	
1974	Shoemaker	10	3	4	
1975	Shoemaker	6	3	2	
1976	Shoemaker	5	7	1	
1977	Shoemaker	8	3	2	
1978	Shoemaker	15	2	1	NCCAA National Champions
1979	Shoemaker	10	6	1	
1980	Shoemaker	18	7	0	NCCAA National Runners-up
1981	Shoemaker	18	2	1	NCCAA National Champions
1982	Shoemaker	14	2	4	NCAA Round of 32
1983	Shoemaker	15	6	1	NCAA First Round
1984	Shoemaker	10	6	2	
1985	Shoemaker	14	3	1	
1986	Shoemaker	17	4	0	NCAA Final 4
1987	Shoemaker	13	4	1	
1988	Shoemaker	18	3	1	NCAA Final 4

1989	Shoemaker	16	4	0	
1990	Shoemaker	16	4	1	
1991	Shoemaker	15	4	1	NCAA Round of 32
1992	Shoemaker	18	4	0	NCAA Round of 16
1993	Shoemaker	15	7	1	NCAA Final 8
1994	Shoemaker	13	5	0	
1995	Shoemaker	19	2	1	NCAA Round of 16
1996	Shoemaker	13	5	1	
1997	Brandt	16	2	3	NCAA Round of 32
1998	Brandt	17	4	1	NCAA Round of 16
1999	Brandt	18	3	1	NCAA Final 8
2000	Brandt	22	2	1	NCAA National Champions
2001	Brandt	21	2	0	NCAA Final 4
2002	Brandt	23	2	1	NCAA National Champions
2003	Brandt	18	2	3	NCAA Round of 16
2004	Brandt	23	2	0	NCAA National Champions
2005	Brandt	24	0	0	NCAA National Champions
2006	Brandt	22	1	2	NCAA National Champions
2007	Brandt	21	3	0	NCAA Final 4
2008	Brandt	22	2	2	NCAA National Champions
2009	McCarty	24	1	0	NCAA National Champions
2010	McCarty	23	1	0	NCAA National Champions

Women's Team, Year-by-Year Results

Year	Coach	W	L	T	Postseason
1988	LaBelle	9	7	0	
1989	Russ	5	6	1	
1990	Russ	9	3	3	
1991	Russ	13	5	0	
1992	Russ	13	4	0	
1993	Russ	10	7	2	
1994	Russ	9	8	0	
1995	Russ	9	8	0	
1996	Russ	6	9	1	
1997	Craig	7	9	1	
1998	Craig	14	3	1	
1999	Craig	13	5	0	
2000	Frey	17	3	0	NCAA Round of 16
2001	Frey	17	1	1	NCAA Round of 16
2002	Frey	23	1	0	NCAA Runner-up
2003	Frey	16	2	3	NCAA Round of 32
2004	Frey	20	1	2	NCAA Final 4
2005	Frey	22	0	1	NCAA National Champions

2006	Frey	18	3	1	NCAA Final 4
2007	Frey	23	1	0	NCAA Runner-up
2008	Frey	24	0	2	NCAA National Champions
2009	Frey	25	0	1	NCAA National Champions
2010	Frey	24	1	0	NCAA Runner-up

Discipline 1

Pursue a Higher Purpose Than Winning

Success Starts by Redefining It

Winning is not the goal. Layton Shoemaker, men's coach 1974-1996

Everybody wants to know the secret, what's in the water. It came from an idealistic vision that was not focused on winning. Dave Brandt, men's coach, 1997-2008

Our goal is not really to win soccer games. But we work really hard at it, without question. Scott Frey, women's coach, 2000-present

We definitely want to win, but it doesn't define us. Our worth as a person is not wrapped up in it. Brad McCarty, men's coach, 2009-present

It's not about winning?

Come on. This is a sport. There's a scoreboard. Each game's outcome is published in the newspaper and online for the whole world to see.

Besides that, in every playoff game, one team moves on and the other packs its boots till the robins return. And in the end, only one team out of more than 400 in Division III hoists a towering trophy that says "National Champions"—a tangible sign of what every team ostensibly desires.

Winning is not the goal? Dave Brandt resides atop a list of NCAA men's soccer coaches with the highest winning percentage. People marvel at Scott Frey's 76-game unbeaten streak and Brad McCarty's two national titles in his first two years. The men's team adds another star to its crest every time they win another championship. This book about the soccer program, for goodness sake, has the word "winningest" in the subtitle!

And still, winning is not the goal?

The Messiah coaches are as unanimous as they are unequivocal. It's not. Beyond that, here's some further audacity: In the words of Coach McCarty, "I think that helps us in the end."

We'll see why later in this chapter. Let's first take a look at their higher purpose than winning.

"Playing for Something More"

In a 2009 interview with *USA Today*, star forward Amanda Naeher claimed: "Our focus is not quite on soccer ... We care about our relationships with each other. We care about our relationship with Christ... (We're) playing for something more."[1]

Something more. Something bigger. It seems to be a common framing over the years.

Savannah (Lehman) Stolzenburg, a 2006 All-American, reflected in a post-graduation letter to her former teammates: "It's not the championship trophy that I miss, but the feeling of being part of something much larger than myself. That is what Messiah soccer is all about." Dave Brandt used similar language in 2005 when describing the men's program: "Being a part of the men's soccer team gives Messiah players the chance to be part of something bigger than themselves."[2]

What is the "something more"? Naeher went on to tell the national media what generations of Messiah soccer alums have said in their day: "You play hard. You play all out all the time for the glory of God, because of what he's given you."

Obviously, in a place that calls itself "Messiah College," God is not a four-letter word, not just a theory, and not tucked away in a sling bag until someone needs him. In fact, quite the opposite. "Many of our athletes" says former Athletics Director Jerry Chaplin, "approach competition as an act of worship," an opportunity to steward the gifts that God has entrusted to them. God is at the center of these kids' lives and as such, at the center of their athletic endeavors.[3]

The same has been true of the coaches, people who consider themselves ambassadors of the faith and disciplers of young leaders. In the women's program, Scott Frey poignantly articulated their core purpose before a coast-to-coast audience in 2002. With CBS Sports cameras in his face prior to the National Championship game, Frey coolly reminded his girls that: "We are playing a sport we love, with teammates we love, for a God we love." It's a line that now rolls off the tongue of most any alumna from the past decade.

It's not the championship trophy that I miss, but the feeling of being part of something much larger than myself.

Savannah (Lehman) Stolzenburg
Class of 2007

Another way Frey has long-described this team is to use words like "family" and "community." In fact, their theme Bible verse for many years has been Acts 4:32: "All the believers were one in heart and mind." That's not intended as a means to the greater end of winning games; "one in heart and mind" is the end in itself. Winning is a byproduct.

A more recent framing, but one that encapsulates the longstanding aspiration of the program, is to be a "team of grace." The Coach explains: "This is something that makes us different. I told them to think about what this team would look like if we became a team of grace—if we simply accepted our teammates, our other friends, everybody within our realm. They're going to mess up. Our team is going to have players that may not train as hard as we'd like them to, maybe they get caught doing something really stupid. It all happens. But because we're a team of grace, that girl's my teammate and that relationship will never, ever change."

It's become a powerful way for them to think about themselves, with many external implications too, as we'll see soon.

Clear framing of their purpose makes a difference on the men's side, as well. Historically, dating back to the Layton Shoemaker days, they talked about "playing for an audience of One," a regular and fitting reminder of what they're really about. During some years, including their pivotal first championship years in 2000 and 2002, this in fact became a mantra, a way to keep them grounded in the face of the escalating media attention.

Relatedly, they remind themselves regularly to put "substance over image"—that is, to ignore what people might say about them, or what's in the paper, or how they're ranked, but instead to concentrate exclusively on their actual mission. Brandt even went so far as to forbid his players from reading Internet posts about D3 soccer, what he calls "the *National Inquirer* of men's soccer." Reading that stuff, he insists, perniciously shifts the team mindset from "substance" to "image," from playing for what really matters to playing for reputation and rankings.

Notice again the point: None of this is about winning games, per se. It's about keeping the team focused on a higher purpose than that, a higher purpose than themselves.

At his first meeting with the team as head coach, Dave Brandt shared his vision of this purpose, an ambition that's had staying power to this day. "I wrote on the board that we were going to be 'the best place in the country to play college soccer.' I didn't say we'd be the best team, I said best place to play, which is controllable. The best guys, the best coaches, the best team chemistry, the best training methods, the best practices, the most positive group."

Troy Sauer was among the first to play for the newly-installed coach and offers this player perspective: "'The best place to play' means you love the guys you're playing with. It means you develop deep relationships that go well beyond soccer. It means you have awesome team chemistry where what the team needs is more important than what you need—and you fully buy-in to that. It means you fight for game time but you don't hold that against your teammate—that you're not mad when you're subbed out, but instead, you're excited for the guy who came in for you. And it means we have each other's back."

It sounds a little like a guy-version of "a team of grace."

Overall, then, it may be accurate to say that the ultimate purpose of these teams—the primary reason they exist—is to *create an environment*, one where people grow and thrive and gratefully represent the One who sent them there. Perhaps that's why the coaches who have stewarded the winningest NCAA soccer program in the past decade can make the paradoxical comment that "it's really not about winning." It's not even primarily about the soccer, they claim.

No, it's about "something more."

Sunday Principles on Monday Afternoon ... and Saturday Night

What does that "something more" look like on a daily basis? Practically speaking, what does all this talk of God and grace and gratitude really mean on Monday afternoon—or, for that matter, Saturday evening under the lights?

Coaches, players, and alumni have answered the question often, though in somewhat different ways across different contexts, from news reports to recruiting materials to alumni breakfasts to book interviews with interloping business professors. But their commentary generally falls into two categories: internal and external implications—how their "higher purpose than winning" applies within the team and how it's expressed to those on the outside.

The Internal Implications: Preparing Students for Life

"It's not just about playing soccer," says Scott Frey. "Players who come out of this program are prepared for life."[3]

Prepared for life. An overstatement? Probably not, but don't take it from me. Listen to the players themselves talk about how the program has changed them:

- "I view people differently. I was pretty judgmental originally. But you learn to accept people for who they are—their flaws, their differences."
- "It revolutionized my idea of how to work hard and why to work hard."
- "I don't think you ever stop growing from your Messiah soccer experience. I'm 49 years old and I'm still growing because of my time at Messiah."
- "This team has largely taught me how to love as Christ does."
- "The person I have become today is the person that I hoped I would become."
- "I get scared sometimes thinking about who I would be if I went anywhere else."

Transformation. Character building. Leadership development. Spiritual formation. *Life preparation*. These are at the center of the soccer program because they're at the center of the College's mission. In fact, at Messiah, athletics is simply one more vehicle by which they happen.

Let's return for a minute to Troy Sauer. He offers an intriguing, personal account of the transformation that's become a Messiah hallmark. Troy, a 2003 grad and currently a middle school teacher and an assistant men's coach at Messiah, claims that: "So many of these principles impact my teaching daily. (The Messiah experience) has made me a better teacher as well as a better husband and father."

It's interesting to note, though, that Troy never really wanted to come to Messiah, a place where his two older brothers played soccer. But in high school, as he was being courted by D1 and D2 schools, Troy had an epiphany when his brother Jake returned home after his first semester at Messiah. "Jake was just different when he came back," Troy remembers. "He was interested in me. He was helping out around the house. He was doing a bunch of things he hadn't done before."

That happens a lot. It's that sort of program.

But character development often takes more than a semester to gain traction. For some athletes it takes years. Men's goalkeeper and current U.S. Four-Man Bobsledding Team Member, Jared Clugston, admits to being a late bloomer in this respect: "I learned that we are here for something so much greater then ourselves. It took me a long time to realize that."

He's carried that perspective forward and his fellow Olympians are taking note. As Jared tells it, he's involved in "a sport that is predominantly track athletes and football players, where everyone is looking out for himself and what's best for him. (However), I have gotten a lot of compliments about my work ethic and my ... team-first attitude."

We are a playing a sport we love
with teammates we love
for a God we love.

Scott Frey
Women's Coach

For athletes on both the men's and women's team, *selflessness*—a challenging attribute for anyone to cultivate—tends to be a natural outgrowth of their deepening faith, their more authentic followership of God during the four-year journey. Almost everyone I interviewed reported that their association with this program grew their faith and consequently, their character. The weekly devotionals, the missions trips and other service activities, and just being around spiritually mature (and maturing) people has a powerful effect. It's in many ways like a healthy small church.

The program prioritizes leadership development as well. "The coaches make leaders out of young men," explains Brett Faro, the 2009 captain. "You can almost see guys start to get it as they go through the program...There's an environment here that fosters leadership. It's unique and it's special."[5]

More specifically, the coaches endeavor to cultivate "servant leadership"—positively influencing others through identifying and meeting needs. Here's a small but representative example. On the men's team, seniors clean up the balls and cones and even hand out water to the guys. During breaks in practice, says All-American Nick Thompson, the seniors jog over first so they can serve the others. Now Nick's doing the same thing as an Assistant Coach at NC State, confusing the team a bit, he chuckles, but modeling the way.

However, it's not just the seniors. And it's not just the men's team. Across these squads every player has some sort of leadership role, a dynamic we'll examine further in Discipline 4, so everyone can begin to develop, through experience, a servant leadership disposition.

Messiah players also grow academically more than they might if they weren't part of the team. Like everything else, this is an intentional part of the program. Both sets of coaches maintain standards like "sit in the front row of all classes (or, if there are no seats there, sit in the middle of the second row), never wear a baseball cap, participate in class and develop a relationship with your teacher that is based first on a student and later as an athlete." Over the years the teams have typically averaged about a 3.2 GPA.

All-Region midfielder Leah Sipe comments on the benefit: "Coming into Messiah I struggled academically, however Coach has never given up on me and this past semester I got a 3.9—the best semester I have ever had."

The Messiah College mission is "to educate men and women toward maturity of intellect, character and Christian faith in preparation for lives of service, leadership and reconciliation in church and society." As we've seen, though, this might just as well be the soccer program's mission. By design, the program changes people and by all accounts, these people are grateful for the change. Center forward Josh Wood said it well, possibly on behalf of many: "I shudder to think about what it would have been like had I gone to another team. It has an impact on you that cannot be measured."

The External Implications: Ambassadors of the Faith

"Playing for something more" has outward expressions as well. As we'll see in a minute, sometimes that's revealed through service to others and sometimes through sportsmanship on-the-field. Sometimes, though, they overtly just put it out there, gently but unabashedly.

A representative case in point: Each year on the eve of the Division III Final Four, the NCAA holds a banquet dinner where a member from each of the four men's teams and the four women's teams gets a few minutes to talk about the team's journey. In 2010, Messiah's Mark Jeschke followed the bold tradition of so many of his predecessors who stood at that podium. Speaking before hundreds of athletes, many who were sizing up each other and day-dreaming about winning it all, Mark chose to abandon any kind of tough-guy image and speak instead about Messiah Soccer's higher purpose.

"When it comes down to it, winning is not ultimately what I or my team play for. We're soccer players, but more importantly to us, we're Christians... Win or lose we compete for the glory of Jesus Christ and we hope to compete in such a way that our faith is evident in our quality and character on and off the field, though unfortunately we don't always do that as well as we'd like to. Of course winning is also a goal, but that's not our purpose. I believe our purpose is found in our faith."

It was a testimony and perhaps a subtle invitation for others to consider their own relationship with God. A poignant moment, but also an echo of the many Messiah men and women who have done the same with their five minutes at the microphone

Ambassadors through Service

More typically, Messiah's witness takes the form of deed rather than word.

Whether it's the men's team tutoring Somali refugee kids in a town near the College or playing futsal (a 5v5 soccer game on a small court) with prisoners in a South American penitentiary, they express their faith through service and relationship-building. So do the women, serving at soup kitchens, cleaning up local parks, playing soccer regularly with girls from inner-city Harrisburg, and even pointing people toward God in Brazil through the quality of their play.

Sometimes, though, the opportunities are no further away than the next dorm room. Says Coach McCarty: "We want our guys to be models for everyone on campus and for the other teams on campus."

The athletes are pro-active about their serving, too, since this is just who they are as people. Consider this illustration of what a "team of grace" looks like, as told by current player Corinne Wulf:

"Last year, Lynchburg's senior goalkeeper, Anna Wright, passed away. This is the goalie that played us in 2009 to a 1-1 tie—the only time we didn't win all season. The Lynchburg women's team raised money for a well in Uganda called 'Anna's Well," since Anna actively worked there ... Our Messiah team raised over $200 to donate to the well formation and sent it to the Lynchburg team with a handwritten letter.

"After playing them this past season, the Lynchburg team gathered around and thanked us for our prayers and support. They told us how much it meant to them and how appreciative they were of the money we donated. Some of them were moved to tears. Then, even though that's not a Christian school, both teams prayed together. It was a unique and very special moment."

The Messiah women did the same for the women's team at Hardin-Simmons University, a Texas team Messiah had, to that point, never played. Their coach, Marcus Wood, related the story to me this way:

"One of our men's soccer players died over spring break in a canoeing accident. The HSU women's team was hurting over this too, but while our men's team received letters of condolences and support from other men's teams, we received only one letter from anyone nationwide and that was from Messiah Women's Soccer—an incredible note with some scripture, saying we know you're struggling because we know how close we are to our men's program. That's a unique quality and ... was so much of a witness to our girls. Wow, this team doesn't even know us and they're taking the time to write us a note from Pennsylvania."

Ambassadors through Sportsmanship

Ironically, Messiah got to know HSU face-to-face later that year in the National Championship game. HSU stunned the Falcons, who hadn't lost in 76 games, fending off a second half onslaught for a 2-1 victory. Coach Wood was duly impressed, admitting to Coach Frey that Messiah reminded him of Barcelona because "we just couldn't get the ball from you." But it was what happened after the game that may have impressed him more. He continued the story:

> "Messiah doesn't experience defeat much, but they were the classiest program in defeat that we ever faced. Even with their streak ending and losing the Championship... everything after the game was complete class. All my girls were saying 'we've never played a team like that.' A lot of teams would be bitter, saying we just bunkered in and played defense to protect the lead. But the Messiah girls were saying 'you deserve it, you're a class act, your team is great, enjoy it'—things that are very difficult to say when you're dealing with your own emotions."

The men's team also has a long history of expressing their faith through sportsmanship, traversing decades. It may, in fact, be among Coach Shoemaker's greatest legacies.

Especially in men's soccer, the more physical team sometimes wins simply by virtue of beating up their opponents. Sure they draw lot more fouls, but that's merely an investment. The dividends are intimidation and opponents' injuries and, not infrequently, victories that may have otherwise been defeats.

Sportsmanship should never be sacrificed for the cause of winning a game— even if it's a championship.

Layton Shoemaker
Men's Coach, 1974-1996

For decades the Messiah teams have shunned that potential advantage. It's not that they won't play a physical game—they certainly do—but they won't play a dirty game, no matter the cost. As they've sometimes said, "form is temporary; class is permanent."

Shoemaker summed up his convictions this way back in 1988 after losing a Final Four game in PKs (13 rounds of them!) and being out-fouled 26 to 5:

> "Is it more important to win a National Championship or to genuinely model good sportsmanship? Obviously, the question will arise: 'Can't we have both?' Yes, I think you can, but sportsmanship should never be sacrificed for the cause of winning a game—even if it's a championship.
>
> "One of the goals of our soccer team is to be good role models of Christian sportsmanship. More specifically, it's to make it through an entire season without receiving any yellow or red cards. This year we were fortunate to have achieved that goal. Twenty-two highly competitive games, posting a record of 18-3-1, and nary a card. Praise God for allowing us to have achieved that distinction."

Shoemaker then shared a further upshot of their 1988 season:

> "The ethics committee of the National Soccer Coaches Association of America and the Intercollegiate Soccer Association of America were so impressed with that achievement (zero yellow cards) that they instituted a Sportsmanship Award to be given annually to the collegiate soccer team that accumulates the fewest cards over the course of the season. Messiah College was honored to be selected as the first recipient of that award. It is a tribute to a fabulous group of young men who accepted the challenge to model good sportsmanship as one evidence of their commitment to principled Christian conduct."[6]

Having read these words in a campus publication, I asked Shoemaker to tell me more about the aftermath of that inimitable 1988 game. He replied: "After that game, some coaches who were there came to me and said you didn't win the game, but you did more than that. You modeled sportsmanship, playing the game the right way. You didn't retaliate. You didn't let it disrupt what you were trying to do. You rose above the occasion."

And what about his team? How did the guys handle the whole idea of non-retaliation and refusing to commit tactical fouls?

"They were 20 years old. They processed it in their own time. The *real* test is what's happening in their life decades later. When they lose a business deal or have some other challenge, how do they handle it? I'm not sure they fully understood it at the time, but the more important thing is to sow the seed for future purposes."

So here we have a convergence of the external and internal—insistence on sportsmanship externally communicates something important to those watching and at the same time, internally develops the character of the Messiah players.

It's no longer the goal of the Messiah teams to complete each season without a card (though they still rarely draw them). It is still the goal, though, and will likely always be, that people see God through them. Playing fairly, with honor and integrity, is a practical, highly-visible outworking of the 'audience of One' and 'team of grace' philosophies. Concludes Corinne Wulf: "Wearing 'Messiah' across our chest, we do our best to represent our God. We do that by showing grace to referees, opposing players, and opposing fans. It is easy to talk back to refs and return rude comments to players and fans. But we believe we can best represent God by showing grace."

There's a higher purpose here, expressed in myriad ways. But a question remains: Might this higher purpose also culminate in higher performance?

Higher Purpose, Higher Performance?

The Messiah coaches have not crafted their lofty, uncommon vision for strategic reasons; they've done so out of a sense of calling. Still, it may generate some competitive advantages that, because they're embedded in the culture, are difficult for other teams to replicate. This is not an exhaustive list, but here are a few of the more formidable ones.

Unity

Foremost, Messiah enjoys the advantage of shared purpose, or unity. Admittedly, that may sound a bit weak: Is something as impalpable as "unity" really an advantage in sports? No less an authority than Coach John Wooden thought so, including it in his basic, three-part formula for success: conditioning, fundamentals, unity.[7] The first two elements are self-explanatory and, relatively speaking, easily achieved; the third is both elusive and extraordinary, a significant distinctive of the best teams in and out of athletics.

Research on "team effectiveness" also shows that unity of purpose makes a difference. The insights of Harvard Business School professor, Jeff Polzer, are typical: "The best teams are those that not only combine the skills of their members to successfully fit the demands of their task, but also energize team members through the bonding that comes with striving toward a common goal."[8]

Much of Messiah's unity, their "striving toward a common goal," flows, of course, out of their worldview, their uniform assumption that they collectively play the game for God rather than for themselves. In doing so, it connects and inspires them. Says 2002 All-American Mindy (Miller) Smith: "Strength comes from unity. By giving yourself to the 'one in heart and mind' philosophy, you will achieve more on and off the field than you ever could alone."

Current captain, centerback Kelsey Gorman, elaborates: "A unified purpose and an understanding that we're all in this together makes you care more for the people around you. As a result, we get upset with ourselves if we make a mistake because we've let down one of our teammates. I don't even want to let a girl get a shot off on my keeper! The offense plays defense for us so we don't have to. Also, when things get tough, this unity and bond helps us so we don't fall apart like other teams do. They start screaming at each other on the field. That doesn't happen with us. We don't get distracted; we stay focused and we play our game."

...and win their games more than 90 percent of the time. Unity has enabled exceptional team chemistry and supercharged their work ethic, something we'll explore thoroughly in Discipline 4.

In this respect, then, *USA Today* may have been mistaken when it reported in 2009: "Playing for God's glory does not help Messiah win, but it does give its teams a unity of purpose."[9] In fact, as it turns out, that unity of purpose may be a key driver of Messiah's dominance on the field.

Alignment

When Dave Brandt initially threw down the gauntlet of being "the best place in the country to play soccer," he did so for a specific and premeditated reason: "Right there I was creating an identity. You're saying 'this is who we are.' Then you can align every attitude and action with that identity... You can just start reigning in people through the recruiting process, through education, or through confrontation sometimes. The neat thing about identity and purpose is when someone runs counter to that you just put it in front of them and what are they going to say?"

A clear and compelling purpose sets the standard and the direction and even the behavioral norms required to get there. That's powerful in and of itself to guide attitudes and actions. But, as Brandt said, it also provides an essential correction device. On any team and in any organization there are those who resist the leader's direction, perhaps even creating subcultures and alternative norms of behavior. That sort of misalignment is toxic as people choose to do their own thing. An advantage for Messiah of having a clear and compelling purpose is that everybody knows it, everybody (at least publicly) agrees that it's good, and when someone deviates from it, coaches, captains or upperclassmen usually just hold the standard before that person.

This sort of alignment mechanism is an intangible asset with an inordinate payoff: *players who ultimately do what the leadership wants done*.

Scott Frey leverages "team of grace" the same way. "Sometimes kids break curfew or don't train the way they should," he explains. "There's always going to be a group who says 'I can't believe she didn't train, that she did this or that.' Even someone's personality can drive you crazy. These things can create a rift.

"What I like about the whole grace thing is that it puts the onus on me, not on you—the onus to accept, to give reconciliation, to say 'it's okay, we still love you and you're still a part of us.' That's a whole different mindset and I think it's huge. And what's great about it for us is that it's so easy to give the reason. Just look at Christ's life: His whole life, his whole being, was grace. Then all they can do is look at you and say yes. There's nothing left to discuss. You don't have to go very far before they simply get it.

"Does that mean we accept or condone the behavior?" Frey asks rhetorically. "No. That's a completely different discussion." But the point here is that for Messiah Soccer, the purpose is in place, the direction is clear, the standard is obvious, and players are held accountable to it. And because they've recruited athletes who are going to fit the culture (Discipline 3), people can just gently remind one another of those standards to reduce the malignant conflicts and power struggles that undermine so many teams.

As you go through the program,
you begin to enjoy other people's successes
more than your own.

Amy Horst
Class of 2010

Selfless, Smarter Play

When it comes to this sport, selflessness may be the oil in the engine. Think about it from the flip side—selfish soccer players dribble too much, they take ill-advised shots, they don't make runs when they're not likely to receive the ball, they bicker with one another, and after 90 minutes, they walk off the field in different directions.

"There are a lot of selfish subtleties that come out on the field if you don't care about the guys on your team," says 2002 All-American and Assistant Men's Coach, Aaron Faro, "like guys not covering for one another because that's not their job. They don't consciously think that, but it happens. Selfish players don't do all the dirty things of playing a game."

Dirty things that, apparently, may help them keep a clean sheet.

Another example comes from Coach McCarty: "When you're yelling at the ref, when you're salty, when you're getting mad, when you're fouling guys in retaliation, you're just thinking about yourself. You're not thinking about the team."

Does that really happen at Messiah? Of course. "There are guys who struggle with these sorts of behaviors,"

McCarty emphasizes. "That's their burden. But I have to help them become self-aware." He does it, among other ways, by pointing to a higher purpose than winning.

So does Scott Frey. For him and the women's program, the attribute is so important that it's listed as their very first "Core Value" in the recruiting packet: "Selflessness means the team comes first. There is no place for selfishness, egotism, or envy." Notice, this is *core value number one*. It's that important. It derives from the higher purpose and culminates in smarter play.

Winning: "Never the Purpose but Always the Point"

They train to win, they step on the pitch to win, they play to win. Students around the Messiah campus wear tee-shirts indicating how often the soccer teams have won. NCAA soccer trophies and larger-than-life photos of postgame celebrations adorn a lengthy hallway that snakes its way through the campus sports complex. Near the playing field, banners that shout "National Champions" can barely fit all the years that's been true.

Symbols of "success" are everywhere. So it should come as no surprise that despite the incessant talk about higher purposes, there's still a tendency, in particular among the younger players, to conceptualize "winning" as the ultimate goal. In one mid-season conversation, for example, after I congratulated one of my students, a sophomore goalkeeper, on the team's string of consecutive shutouts, he responded first with appreciation but then with a rejoinder: "It won't mean anything if we don't win the National Championship." In another conversation, a 2003 grad reflected on a playoff loss ten years ago and wondered aloud: "Why was I so consumed by that?"

Christians on the athletic field are often viewed as soft. We don't treat our task that way. Jesus didn't just go around hugging school children. He was also on a mission.

Troy Sauer
Class of 2003, Assistant Men's Coach

The coaches both affirm and temper this sort of passion. Says Scott Frey, "Let's be honest, winning does matter. Soccer always comes back to soccer. But in the big picture, we realize those successes are momentary. The next day you're back to work."

The men's coaches also address the tension regularly, offering the boys wisdom refined in the crucible of experience. On one hand, they say, it's a game so we shouldn't be apologetic about wanting to win. Assistant Troy Sauer frames this theologically: "Christians on the athletic field are often viewed as soft. We don't treat our task that way. Jesus didn't just go around hugging school children. He was also on a mission." And Coach Brandt puts it almost poetically: "Winning is never the purpose, but always the point. I mean, it *is* athletics."

But on the other hand, it's not just athletics, as he's quick to point out. At Messiah, soccer is also a ministry—a ministry that's cultivated legions of servant leaders. A ministry that quietly but intentionally reflects God's love. And a ministry that prepares people for life, instilling in them core values and clear perspective about what matters the most.

"If at the end of your career," wrote Frey to his team in a 2010 email, "all you can say is 'I was a National Champion and we won a lot of games,' then I'd say it wasn't worth the time and energy. But if you can look back and say 'I learned a lot about myself. I did things I never thought possible, both physically and psychologically. I made the most important and lasting friendships of my life. I've learned that helping others and seeing them succeed at something is better than having it happen to me,' then it is without question worth all that you do."

Indeed, at Messiah, soccer is a ministry that's achieved unprecedented success by first redefining it.

Appendix to Discipline 1

Messiah Soccer Core Values

The Women's Team

1. The team comes first. There is no place for selfishness, egotism, or envy.

2. We have complete control over our physical preparation and take responsibility for it.

3. We choose to be positive.

4. There are no unimportant details. We do things a certain way for a reason. "Little things make big things happen."

5. We mean no offense and take no offense with each other.

6. Team Spirit: An *eagerness* to sacrifice personal interests or glory for the welfare of all.

7. Success: Giving of your best at all times, no matter the circumstances.

8. We work hard.

9. Do the right thing, for the right reason, all the time.

10. We are a team of grace.

The Men's Team

1. We dare greatly.
2. We work hard.
3. We choose to be positive.
4. We mean no offense and take no offense with each other.
5. We show no weakness.
6. We finish strong.
7. We walk like champions.
8. We support the team mission regardless of our circumstance.
9. We are a collection of friends first, and soccer players second.
10. We seek excellence in all areas, not just soccer.
11. We seek to play a role in our local and international communities.
12. We want our four year experience to have "an unspeakable impact" on our lives.

Discipline 2

Be Intentional About Everything

There's More Under Your Control Than You Realize

As the bus wheels turned toward the stadium for the 2008 National Championship game, Coach Brandt's mental wheels were also turning. "I knew the game was going to be a stalemate," he recalls with a slight head shake, "so I considered going to a 3-5-2 formation."

Messiah's staple was a 4-3-3, with an occasional 4-4-2 to throw opponents off-balance. They had won five titles with it. So a formation change, especially at this point, was a radical thought. But Brandt was never one to stand still. "I was always looking for some strategic advantage that allows us to win by four. I'll gamble to get that advantage."

On the bus, he floated the 3-5-2 idea past Assistant Brad McCarty. Brandt chuckles about the response: "Brad looked at me, rolled his eyes and said, 'Dave … come on.' And that was it. We played our system."

It wouldn't be Brandt's last radical thought for the day, though.

His instincts could not have been more accurate. After 90 minutes of regulation and two overtimes, a stalemate.

Messiah and Stevens, the two best D3 teams in the country, remained knotted at one goal apiece. PKs would settle it.

Brandt's easy call was who his five shooters would be. The harder call was which keeper to send in. At breakfast that morning, he had huddled with his brain trust of McCarty and his two keeper coaches, Dustin Shambach and Aaron Schwartz. The group recommended senior back-up keeper Nick Blossey, who had emerged as a PK connoisseur. Now, in the moment of truth, the contingency would become reality. Brandt had asked Blossey to warm up during the second OT; now he sent him in, despite Nick having not played a solitary minute during the entire playoff run—a full 28 days.

"It was an objective call," Brandt asserts. "We just thought Bloss was uncanny on PKs."

After Messiah's captain, J.D. Binger, netted their initial attempt, the Stevens shooter went high to the left. But Blossey was there first, using all of his six-foot-two-inch frame to push it wide. Messiah's Geoff Pezon drilled an unstoppable shot for their second goal. The Stevens shooter who followed went right, only to be again stymied by a two handed save.

A Messiah miscue on their third shot gave Stevens some life. At the twelve now stood the man who had scored their dramatic equalizer late in regulation. He hit a wicked worm burner to the lower left corner, a spot many lanky keepers can't reach. But Blossey was "uncanny" again, reading it all the way, nabbing it from the nylon.

Three consecutive PK stops when everything was on the line. Simply unprecedented. Messiah's Nick Thompson coolly but almost anticlimactically converted the next shot for the Falcons, securing their sixth title in nine years.

It was among the greatest moments in the storied history of Messiah soccer. But—and this is the point for our purposes—it didn't exactly happen by chance. They meticulously trained for it.

Intentionality may be the biggest part of our success.

Dave Brandt
Men's Coach, 1997-2008

"Some people don't believe you can practice PKs, but you can," said a jubilant Blossey after the smoke cleared. "We've been training for this over the last four or five weeks."[10] In fact, Messiah had been training for them more deliberately since exiting the NCAA tournament on PKs in 2003.

Keeper coach Dustin Shambach, who himself was an impressive PK stopper as a Messiah player, was Blossey's primary teacher, working closely with him on how to read shooters—what to watch about their hips and their shooting foot—as well as the philosophy of waiting long enough to never dive the wrong way. They worked on it a lot during the playoff run.

But let's face it: This type of training isn't unusual. Most teams now train for shootouts during the post-season. Physically, at least. Technically. They practice the mechanics of scoring and stopping shots. The more instructive part of the backstory may be that Coach Brandt went further than this, ensuring the *mental preparation* of Blossey and all his other reserve players. He made it a priority.

"Coach always wanted us ready," Blossey recalls. "He'd often remind us: 'If I turn to you and tell you to go in, you should not be surprised ... I also remember Coach telling us a story along these lines about a little boy, a story that stayed with me throughout all of my preparation. It was really inspirational."

That tale was about Abraham Lincoln studying by the pine log fire at night, thinking about the possibility of being President someday. As the story goes, Lincoln's perspective, and one of his most prophetically quotable lines, was: "I will study and get ready, and perhaps my chance will come."

Whether that story was true or legend didn't matter to Blossey. It was motivating. He made that line his own and kept working hard, learning, pushing himself and his teammates to "get ready," just as Coach wanted him to do, in the hope that his chance would come. All the reserve players did, which, according to Nick, gave him even more impetus: "To see a guy continuing to bust his butt even though he's not getting rewarded for it on the field, that's inspiring. And it upholds what we're all about."

Now admittedly, against the backdrop of the shootout heroics, these training specifics may sound a bit mundane, but that's actually part of the lesson, too. *Intentionality in everything, including the little things, makes the big things more possible*.

Some of these "things" at Messiah are conventional, like setting aside time for PK training. Others are less commonly practiced across soccer programs, like retaining a second keeper coach in case the first one can't make it. And some are downright rare, like managing the mindset of reserve players, ensuring their readiness through reminders that they matter, and even tracking down inspirational stories to energize them. From the biggest, most obvious things to the smallest details, the Messiah coaches are intentional and they're assiduous.

How important is that habit? Does it really payoff? And what, exactly, does that look like in operation? Let's look closely at what may be one of Messiah's primary secrets to success in both the men's and women's program.

"If You Don't Like What's Happening on Your Team, It's Your Fault"

Here's the starting point. Coach Brandt is blunt about it when speaking to an audience of coaches or other leaders: "If you don't like what's happening on your team, it's your fault."

It's a simple, forthright statement. But it carries with it a pivotal assumption, one that may be a game-changer for leaders everywhere: As the leader, you have the power—all the power you need, in fact—so use it to create the team and the culture you really want.

Whether you realize it or not, continues the Coach, almost everything is under your control. Don't whine about uninspired team members, or a culture of mediocrity, or people who won't follow, or your anemic pipeline of recruits. Those things, like almost everything else, are controllable. Shapeable. Changeable. You're in charge, now do something about it.

And set aside the ubiquitous excuse that you don't have enough of a budget. "Our recruiting budget when I left (in 2008) was $800 per year," says Brandt, a number that may be more stunning when we learn about their remarkable recruiting system in the next chapter. "It's part of my basic philosophy, though: I don't need favors, I don't need outside help. Coaches who do don't get it done. I just need a team to coach."

It may all sound a bit brusque, but the real question is whether it's true. Does the leader really have that much power and control over the outcomes?

In the Messiah soccer program, they have no doubt. And that culminates in a broader ethos of individual responsibility that pervades the program. Consider, for example, a core value for the women: "We have complete control over our physical preparation and take responsibility for it." It's a choice. So own it.

In the same vein, Frey is plainspoken in his recruiting packet: "We are all products of the choices we make every second of every day." He then shares a longstanding adage: "If you want to know why your life is the way it is today, look at what you did yesterday. If you want to know what your life will be like tomorrow, look at what you are doing today."

So with regard to leadership, the assumption that you have the power means that you also have the responsibility. As such, it's an assumption that affects almost everything. Brandt offers the example of "how prepared as a coach we are for practice." Designing the practice, linking it to the match, making sure things are in order well ahead of time—"every little action matters." And once we realize this, he concludes, it's "an end to laziness" because as a coach or as a player, you now have to "take responsibility for every single thing you do."

Indeed, the leadership steps up to that challenge. Coach Frey says it plainly: "There's not much we don't orchestrate."

No Unimportant Details

That points to an essential corollary to this intentionality principle. As it says in the women's core values, "There are no unimportant details." For Messiah soccer, there's an unremitting, painstaking thoroughness in all that they do—a seeming obsession with the little things.

At a 2009 press conference after the Messiah men's semi-final victory, a reporter asked Coach McCarty, tongue in cheek: "It's your first year (as head coach) and you're in the National Championship game. It's always gonna be this easy, right?"

McCarty's serious response to the not-so-serious question captures the corollary: "We try not to think about that. We try to focus on the small details and that gets us to where we want to go."

His assistant coaches are similarly fixated, having seen the merits of meticulousness when they were players. Says Troy Sauer: "First and foremost, there's absolutely no magic to what we do. We work hard and we work hard at small things—doing the little things really, really well." His peer Aaron Faro also puts it cogently: "A mantra around here is 'if anything matters, everything matters.'"

Intentionality, all the way down to the details. Importantly, it's not just the leaders' philosophy, but one the players themselves embrace. Current senior Leah Sipe is representative and quite specific about what this means in daily life:

> "Talent doesn't and won't ever be the factor that sets you apart. When you are at the Final Four, everyone is talented, everyone can play. There needs to be another factor that sets you apart. For us, it is being detailed in all aspects of our lives.
>
> "It means eating healthy food, because that's what's better for the cause. It means getting in my run even though it's hot outside, because my team is worth it. It means getting my homework done because we have a night game or we'll be traveling for NCAA's. It means notifying our professors that we won't be in class because of our away game. It means getting to bed on time every night because sleep makes a difference on the field. It means showing God's grace to our opponents and spreading love around campus. It means practicing the way we play and perfecting the system.

"The little details on the off the field are what makes Messiah soccer what it is."

Through Leah's words, one of the team's core values reverberates: "There are no unimportant details. We do things a certain way for a reason. 'Little things make big things happen.'"

Now, having said that, Coaches Brandt, Frey and McCarty are unanimous that even though most aspects of their system are controllable, "winning" is not.

McCarty says it well: "There are things we can control and things that we can't. I can't control whether we go to another Final Four or whether we win another National Championship. Soccer's a funny game. You can dominate and lose 1-0."

Every soccer coach understands that statement. In this sport, winning is not under our power. So McCarty instead takes the pragmatic path: "What we *can* do is cling to the principles that Dave provided us and that got us where we are today." One of those principles is that almost everything else *is* within a leader's purview, so incessant intentionality will make winning more likely.

There are no unimportant details.
We do things a certain way for a reason.
Little things make big things happen.

From the Core Values of the Women's Team

Says Brandt, unequivocally, you have more control than you realize over what happens with your kids, and in leading your church, and in running your sports camps, and in improving your business, and in cultivating great students, and with the soccer team you lead. "That doesn't mean insisting on four practices a week for fifth graders, but it does mean you don't just cross your fingers. Intentionality may be the biggest part of our success."

Of all the contributing factors, that's really saying something. So let's take a more granular and highly-practical look at some further examples of what this means in the Messiah program.

Incessant Intentionality: Some Further Examples

They do almost everything on purpose. Their whole system is designed and deliberate. Attention to detail touches every element of the Messiah Method and then some. These coaches are incessantly intentional. Here's just a sampling of their approach, roughly corresponding to the disciplines covered in this book.

Intentionality in Communicating the Purpose

This is no small matter. Messiah soccer coaches, past and present, have been quite deliberate about keeping in front of players the purposes and principles of the program. Layton Shoemaker was the forerunner, often beginning a talk with "Today's principle is..." His pupils Brandt, Frey and McCarty carry on this vision-casting tradition (though with distinctively different styles. For instance, according to McCarty, "When Dave wrote an email it was a book; when I write one it's two lines.")

Regarding the women's program, current captain Kelsey Gorman shares this insight about Scott Frey: "Coach often shares something with us from books he's reading or emails he's getting, always reminding us of the themes—especially when we're about to go compete with one another. And that's very intentional because that's the most threatening aspect to our relationships."

One of the "themes" to which Kelsey refers is "competition and grace," something Frey emphasizes a lot before their unsparing practices in an effort to preempt strife. At other times he focuses, often by email, on whatever might be most relevant to the girls: excellence in school work (near finals period), smart decisions on the field (during the season), preparation (during the summer training months), getting to bed on time (which is always topical for college students). Kelsey, like her current and former teammates, has found these emails helpful and has saved many for future inspiration.

Frey has even gone so far as to ask soccer alumnae to write letters to the current team about what they miss most, something that invigorates the team through perspective. Like his colleagues, he's made a priority of keeping the vision and principles and higher purpose before everyone all the time.

Leadership expert John Kotter, from Harvard Business School, popularized the notion that most leaders under-communicate their vision by a factor of ten.[11] The Messiah coaches work hard to ensure they're not among them.

Intentionality in the Recruiting Visit

Nowhere is the Messiah leadership more intentional, it seems, than in creating a unique experience for prospects. Both the men's and women's programs work hard at this, essentially choreographing the visit from beginning to end.

Unlike so many other soccer programs that merely toss a recruit to a couple freshman and hope they have a good weekend, at Messiah, the recruiting visit is an all-hands-on-deck event. In advance of the visit, emails fly around to the players, introducing the recruit and coordinating the schedule. Coaches match the recruit to a roommate who has similar interests or academic focus. They also assign specific, high-profile players to escort the parents around campus. And then, the whole team hangs out together with the recruit for a significant part of the weekend.

"It's really helpful," says Kelsey Gorman, "because it lets the recruits see how close we really are and how well we get along. It also shows them that Messiah is a different place."

Her coach readily concurs: "If I can get somebody on campus, I have a good chance. The visit is what really sells them. The interaction of teammates is so impressive." As we'll see in Discipline 3, there's a plethora of evidence to back up his belief.

Intentionally in Relationship-Building

Messiah players spend *a lot* of time together, whether they want to or not (but for the record, it's usually the former).

During preseason they're not just training physically and technically, they're canoeing and camping and doing a ropes course and attending worship services as a team. During the rest of the year, they gather regularly to play cards or to go duckpin bowling or to play board games at the coach's house. Service activities and missions trips also adorn the off-season.

It all contributes to the extraordinary team chemistry, a hidden asset many coaches know is essential but struggle to attain. Like everything else in these programs, though, at

Messiah they don't just hope that it happens. They cultivate chemistry by design.

Growing any type of relationship requires time. There's no shortcut. So at Messiah, much of this team time is mandated and proactively coordinated by coaches or captains, in particular on the guys' side where it's less likely to happen naturally. There's no opting out, no "I don't feel like it," no "sorry, I have plans to go home this weekend." And admittedly, the mandate occasionally leaves a trail of disgruntled girlfriends or boyfriends or even parents in its wake. But as we'll explore in Discipline 4, this "forced family fun" as they call it, is instrumental for cultivating the unique chemistry that keeps these players working their hardest for one another.

Intentionality in Customizing Practice

"I'm a legal pad guy," says Dave Brandt. "I have no practices saved anywhere for 12 to 14 years. I almost consciously don't keep records of this stuff. It forces me to work."

This is an unusual habit, and quite an inefficient one. But when managing a soccer team, like managing almost anything else, there is often a tradeoff between efficiency and effectiveness. For the Messiah coaches, the latter always takes precedence.

"I just *agonize* over practice," he reveals, more expressively than usual. "Rarely does it just come. I'll spend two hours at night and I'm embarrassed to say sometimes I get stuck at work and I'll just lose a day in trying to come up with a practice. You can't function doing this very often, but I wrestle with it. It's hard."

This is not a matter of finding innovative, new drills or some novel, draconian fitness regimen. Rather, the goal, as we'll unpack more fully in Discipline 5, is to train in a way that actually affects game day performance. An enormous advantage that Messiah enjoys is that there's an inextricable link between training and the match. But to retain that link, coaches are constantly and exhaustingly reinventing their training methods.

Coach Frey is no different. "I used to keep my practice notes, but I never used them later. I didn't even know where they were." Instead, like Brandt, he regularly reinvents his training based on the current situation and need. "Some days (the practice I'm designing) just doesn't feel right. I'll go see Brad or I'll call Davey to get ideas. How do I get my sixes and eights running in the next game? How do I train that?"

I just agonize over practice.
Rarely does it just come.

Dave Brandt
Men's Coach, 1997-2008

Historically, Brandt and Frey have been not only prepared, but punctilious. Assistant Men's Coach Aaron Faro indicates that not much has changed in this regard during the recent McCarty years: "The coaching staff is at the field early and has everything laid out. We have a plan on paper regarding who's going to be in what group for certain drills. We set up our cones straight. We make sure we have enough balls. All coaches know what their responsibilities are for a given practice. Guys jog in for their water and jog back out and we stay on the time schedule. We never come to the end of a week saying 'weren't we going to work on this?' It all gets done because we planned it out ahead of time."

They even think through the ebbs and flows of the practice, compensating for the energy and enthusiasm that's sometimes lost as the practice unfolds. Continues Faro: "Guys have limited focus after a day of classes, so we stay on top of this or we may start to lose them. We often design the last part of practice to keep their interest and focus."

"(Preparing practice) does take a big portion of my day," admits McCarty. "It's a grind and it's not easy." Why work so hard to build customized practices? Brandt speaks for all the Messiah coaches when he responds: "Because I believe it matters. Every minute of practice matters. And I've been able to convince our teams of that, too."

Intentionality in Preparing Game Day Talks

"Fight for it with all your heart and soul because *nobody* is going to hand it to you. Calvin is *not* going to hand it to you just because you have Messiah on your chest. Let's go earn it boys!"

In the locker room, the guys are focused. Coach McCarty is animated. The CBS cameras are rolling and the 2009 Championship game is about to begin.

Messiah coaches don't talk long before a game, but that doesn't give them license to wing it. They build their pregame talk ahead of time. Then they sometimes re-build it. This needs to be right.

"I'm very intentional about this," says Coach Frey. "I have some key points I want to make and I write them down. I only talk to them for five or ten minutes before a game, but I want to trip their trigger."

To do that, Frey won't just cover X's and O's or the specifics of the game plan. The team knows all that by now anyway. Instead, well in advance he's taken the time to identify a theme for the day—complacency, greatness, playing to a standard of excellence—and to find an illustrative story or maybe some quotes that are inspirational and on-point. He knows exactly where he's going with those five minutes.

"Then, it's semi-rehearsed," he continues. "In my head, I've gone over what I want to say several times."

It may seem like an inordinate amount of work for such a brief moment, but again, *it matters,* as we'll see further in Discipline 6. The reality is this: It often requires more preparation to speak persuasively for five minutes than it does for 15 or 20 minutes. In the same way that great teachers distinguish themselves by preparation that exceeds their peers, these coaches also invest the necessary time to choreograph their game day communication.

Intentionally Confronting Mediocrity

"I can pick out two percent of going through the motions and I won't have it." Coach Brandt is as unflinching as he is unapologetic about this issue, and his players know it. No one wants to test his resolve.

Why such tenacity? It goes back to individual responsibility. "This is under the player's control," asserts Brandt. "I'm a reasonable person. I'm not going to ask you for anything you can't do. I'm not asking you to be Pele; I'm not asking you to be perfect. I'm asking you to give your best at all times. These guys get it."

Some leaders don't, though, succumbing to the temptation to accommodate mediocrity. It's understandable. Addressing under-performance, especially when it might only be "two percent of going through the motions," risks relationships. It risks the leader's popularity. It makes everyone uncomfortable. More than that, it's arduous, says Brandt: "Confronting the human tendency to be comfortably mediocre is exhausting. It's a battle in leadership."

A battle that Brandt unfailingly chooses to engage, as we'll see throughout the book. The Coach pushes people toward their full potential, without regard for his personal reputation, an approach that has helped his teams repeat and three-peat as national champs. It also helps turn boys into remarkable, young men.

... and girls into dedicated, young women. When asked how long they'll typically do a drill, Kelsey Gorman responded, "If we do it well, maybe 20 minutes. If it's not good, we do it till we get it right."

There's wisdom in that approach. Though he has a very different personality from Dave Brandt, Scott Frey similarly insists that his players continually strive to perform their best—and strive to stay a step ahead of the competition. "When we're in front," he says about Messiah being atop the national rankings, "I'm running like crazy to stay there ... I want to do things this year in our training that we didn't do last year. So I'm going to push them. It's been an ongoing process of little things, little pushes that create this culture (of continuous improvement.)"

Which brings us back full circle to getting the details right. At Messiah, you'll find players who receive the ball with the correct foot, who have a great first touch, who know their passing options and hit their targets, who give maximum effort in every practice and on every drill, and who do a hundred other things with habitual precision.

Why? Because at Messiah, you'll find coaches who are never soft on players going through the motions.

***If we do a drill well, we do it for maybe 20 minutes.
If it's not good, we do it till we get it right.***

**Kelsey Gorman
Class of 2012**

Intentionality in Relating to Players

I said to Dave Brandt in our interview: "Your players have described you in a lot of ways, almost all of them lavishly complimentary, but one also used the term 'shrouded in mystery.' How close do you let your players get to you?"

His response pointed toward one other issue that he manages purposefully, one with which many leaders wrestle:

> "I'm an introvert, so I'm not easily buddy-buddy with people. But I always overtly mean to have a good and healthy relationship with every player. And I'll always do something about it if I feel it's in jeopardy at any moment.
>
> "Sometimes there's an element of separateness to leadership. You want to be a little elusive and a step ahead. But that's not how I relate to my assistant coaches. I don't need to keep any professional distance there. There's a level of transparency with the assistants that I don't necessarily want with my players."

How does a leader balance buddy and boss? Ally and administrator? Friend and "freakishly good coach"?

Deliberately, according to Brandt. "For the most part, this is all very intentional, the management of these relationships and the dynamic between me and the team. I'm relational, but clearly in charge" (a style we'll examine further in the last chapter, "Some Other Enabling Conditions of Success.")

In fact, he eschews the whole idea of seeking some sort of "balance" or compromise between these seemingly competing options. "Leaders are trying to figure out where to place these scales," he explains with two flat hands in the air, one much higher than the other. He moves the top hand down slightly and the bottom hand up slightly, but nowhere near parallel, and tells me, "Leaders say 'okay, just right.'" Then Brandt resets his hands to their original spots and says, "No, my approach is," he gradually moves both his flat hands as high as he can reach: "okay, just right."

It's an intriguing "both-and" concept, but it's one to which Frey and McCarty also subscribe. Their objective, sometimes realized, sometimes merely aspirational, is to be *both* the discipler *and* the disciplinarian, trading off nothing.

"Lombardi was spot on with respect to this," concludes Brandt, citing one of his role models. "Do I become more compassionate by being less results-driven? No. Balance is not the answer. A leader has to be both." Intentionally.

The Lifeblood of Leadership

Almost any leader can do this, taking their team to the next level of excellence—at least any leader who's this committed.

It starts with a clear and compelling vision of the future, something that you and those around you care about deeply. It then continues with the energizing recognition that as a leader, you have control over just about everything, much more than you might realize.

Intention naturally follows. And so does *industriousness*, the lifeblood of leadership.

It's been implicit throughout this chapter, but consider how hard these coaches work. Nothing happens by chance in these programs. Coaches never just hope for the best. And despite Messiah being a Christian college, no one claims that their championships are some miraculous work of divine providence. Rather, as many of my interviewees mentioned when asked about the success: "It's harder than it looks"—harder than one can possibly imagine from the stands or the sports pages. Daily and doggedly, the Messiah leadership exemplifies the work ethic necessary to develop a preeminent team and then to sustain it.

That ethic has become a lifestyle for them. Even for something that doesn't affect the team directly, like when Dave Brandt teaches other coaches, his commitment is exemplary and sometimes unique. One D3 coach told me that although the National Soccer Coaches Association of America (NSCAA) Annual Convention attracts famous speakers from all over the world, Brandt's session before several hundred coaches was the best he had ever seen. "Dave just prepared more than anyone else," said Marcus Wood, the 2010 Division III Women's Coach of the Year. "It was exceptional."

They're always driving, always reflecting, always strategizing and problem-solving and reinventing. Brandt spends hours at home with a legal pad, sketching out formations and passing patterns, only to have most of them land on the floor crumpled up. At Messiah he'd regularly sit through obligatory department meetings getting real work done—working on drills and training plans. It's practically an obsession; his mind never stops.

It's true of Scott Frey as well. Says Erin Hench, 2009 National Player of the Year: "Coach Frey puts in so much effort behind the scenes that fans will never see, but they certainly see the effects of it." And that work happens just about everywhere. Frey laughs about what his life has become: "I'm doing my gardening at home thinking 'what if we did this?' Almost every moment of my day I'm thinking about this team."

Their mentor, Layton Shoemaker, set the standard for industriousness, running the soccer program, the athletic department, an academic department, and teaching classes—often in the same semester! Former player Barry Goodling, now a Messiah VP, recalls: "The guy was a workaholic. Nobody spent more hours at Messiah than Layton."

This is what it takes to be the best, leaders who are tireless and tenacious. Coach McCarty, who's also a full-time dad, is in fact keeping Messiah atop D3 with four young kids in tow. But each Messiah coach will tell you that they love what they're doing and wouldn't have it any other way. Frey may speak for the lot of them when he effervesces: "I love coming to the office. It's not work to me. My wife asks 'are you ever going to take a day off?' and I say 'Why? *Every day* is a day off!'"

We know the results. All this effort and intentionality pays handsomely, from creating a genuine "team of grace" to becoming "the best place in the country to play soccer" to life-changing mentorship of 20 year olds to transforming "The Final Four" into "The Final Three Plus Messiah." It even kept a back-up keeper—one who had spent 28 days on the bench—mentally-prepared to thwart three straight penalty kicks.

As it turned out, this was Dave Brandt's last call as Messiah's head coach. He accepted a job with the Naval Academy that same month. Fitting that it was a brilliant call and the culmination of a rigorous and quite intentional process.

Discipline 3

Recruit the "Both-And" Players

Why Talent is Not Enough

December 2010. San Antonio again for the Final Four, just like last year. The Messiah and Lynchburg men had dispatched their semi-final opponents and now squared off for what many expected would be yet another clinical Messiah victory.

Only nobody told Lynchburg. They battled the two-time defending champs to a scoreless draw in the first half and then stunned them with fifteen to go in the match on a blistering shot to the upper 90 from outside the box. Coach McCarty sent in every starter who was resting on the bench but eight minutes later, Messiah still had no tallies. Then McCarty replaced a defender with a forward. The Falcons' moment came in the 85th minute when that very forward, Dan Squire, deftly settled a towering, 70-yard clearance from Messiah keeper Jake Berry, held off a centerback and toe-poked in the equalizer.

It would be settled in overtime. Messiah's forte. But again, nobody informed Lynchburg who quickly put the Falcons on their heels. Berry came up huge with a reaction save at the lower left corner. A minute later, Messiah countered. Midfielder and D3 Player of the Year, Geoff Pezon, received the ball 40 yards from Lynchburg's goal. Target man Danny Thompson instinctively sprinted outside, pulling a defender with him, creating just enough space for Pezon to beat his man and bury the dramatic game winner from the 18.

It was Messiah's eighth national title in eleven years and among the greatest moments in program history. Some might suggest, though, that what followed was even greater.

Fast-forward a week or so to a celebrating Messiah men's team, enjoying a Christmas party in the atrium of an academic building. From her office nearby, Dean Sue Hasseler could hear the festivities and saw a perfect opportunity. One of her faculty members, Terry Earhart, lay in a hospital bed struggling with mesothelioma, a rare and ruthless form of cancer. Sue wanted to send Terry, an avid soccer fan who had followed the teams for decades, one of the newly-minted, "2010 National Champions" tee-shirts, ideally a shirt signed by all of the players. And there were all the players, practically at her door. Problem was, she didn't yet have one of those tee-shirts, so she asked a team member if she could have the one he was wearing and replace it later.

"I can do better than that." The offer came from Pezon as he pulled a soccer ball out of his sling bag and handed it to the Dean. "Give him this."

The ball already had all the signatures on it. And in fact, it was the championship game ball that Pezon's teammates had signed and given to him only a few minutes earlier.

A titanic act of compassion, indeed, but it gets even better: Geoff Pezon had never met Professor Earhart. He had just heard of the professor's plight and in that moment, he thought he could lend an assist.

The timing of the gift was equal to the timing of Pezon's goal. After weeks in the hospital, Terry had just learned that post-surgery complications would prevent his discharge, perhaps past Christmas. "When the doctor came in to my room and told me I may not be home for Christmas...that was my lowest point," recalls Terry. Then, that same afternoon, literally hours after receiving the crushing news, the package from campus arrived.

"When I opened that box and saw the game ball," Terry continued, effervescing at the memory, "I'm not ashamed to say I cried. The timing of receiving that ball was perfect and so meaningful to me. It represented a real turning point in my recovery. I believe it was the Lord's timing."

Geoff was nonchalant when asked by a campus reporter about the extraordinary gift. "Everything we learn here emphasizes 'team over individual' and putting others before ourselves. When I heard of Professor Earhart's hard circumstances, I definitely wanted to do anything I could to help. I'm just happy I could put into practice what the faculty and coaches at Messiah have taught me."[12]

What They're Looking For: Messiah's Recruiting Philosophy

Messiah College is a "both-and" place. While elevating faith to a paramount ideal, it does the same with intellect. While affirming the value of discipline, it affirms the value of imagination. While seeking harmony among people, it respects and even celebrates difference. While maintaining that absolute truth exists and is knowable, it also allows students to think broadly for themselves to pursue it.

The College takes criticism from many in the faith for being too liberal and inclusive in its theology. It takes criticism from many outside the faith for being too conservative and exclusive, even dogmatic. But for the record, Jesus heard the same criticisms. Such is the plight of a "both-and" Christian institution that's striving to be faithful, a College that sincerely embraces the vertical dimension of the faith traditionally emphasized by the right and the horizontal dimension of the faith traditionally emphasized by the left.

Along its broad, brick sidewalks, there are now tangible examples of the "both-and" character everywhere on campus. Banners (more specifically, "ligatures") adorn its light posts, each containing two words—two ideals—that at first glance might seem incompatible. But the words are joined together in an artistic way, representing their connectedness, the aspiration of Messiah to affirm *both* the first ideal *and* the second. Among the word pairs on these ligatures are discovery-belief, humility-aspiration, planet-village, work-play, and options-decisions. Not either-or at Messiah. Both-and.

It will come as no surprise, then, that the athletics motto at the College has the same bifold quality to it: "Pursuing athletic excellence, developing Christian character." Neither objective by itself is sufficient, as its Web site explains: "If we don't accomplish both of these goals in a season, then we have not had a successful season."

Pursuing athletic excellence, developing Christian character ... If we don't accomplish both of these goals in a season, then we have not had a successful season.

From the Messiah College Athletics Web Site

Which brings us back to the soccer program and to the remarkable benevolence of Geoff Pezon. He personifies the "both-and" ideal. A few months later, he surprised everyone again, having been offered a pro contract under the provision that he be available immediately after his May 2011 graduation. But Geoff wanted to join his teammates at that time for a two-week missions trip to Columbia, a request the pro team rejected. As Geoff tells it, "I thought it would be more beneficial to serve than to play professionally at the time." So in a leap of faith, he turned down the contract and boarded the plane for South America.

Todd Suessmuth, a soccer stud during the 1980s who currently co-owns the Messiah goal scoring record, also traveled with the team to Columbia. Afterward he told me: "Geoff's a great student, a great person, a giver, down to earth. You'd never know he was the Player of the Year by just talking to him. He talks about 'team' and about 'us,' not about himself or what he did this year." Teammate Josh Wood echoed the "both-and" quality of Geoff, adding: "Pezon may be the best D3 player in the nation but he's the goofiest player on the team. He has so much fun being around everyone else. He's everybody's best friend. But on the field he's totally serious. No one works harder."

Apparently, the pro club also valued his skill and work ethic. In a delightful epilogue to this story, when Geoff returned from Columbia, the club still wanted him to anchor the center of their midfield.

There have been plenty of other "both-and" players at Messiah. Amanda Naeher is representative on the women's side, though we could name so many others. Amanda, as you might recall from the Purpose chapter (Discipline 1) is the young women who shared so poignantly with the national media that she and her teammates play for "something more" than winning, in particular, to please God. She's pleases the crowd as well, having put the ball in the net a jaw-dropping 108 times in four years and being twice named the D3 Player of the Year. Amanda even earned a spot on the "NCAA Division III All-Silver Anniversary Team," honoring her as one of the best 11 players of the past 25 years.

"Both-And" players. Players of competence and character. Great players with small egos who want to be part of something bigger than themselves. They're out there and Messiah gets them. And as we'll see shortly, it creates a competitive advantage.

"The Genius of the And"

These are hardly anomalous examples. Kacie Klynstra, another member of the ultra-exclusive D3 Silver Anniversary Team, and Kai Kasiguran, a four-time All-American who went on to play professionally for the Chicago Fire, are two more illustrations of *both* talent *and* humility (not to mention some pretty cool alliteration). Klynstra, for example, as phenomenal as she was locking down attackers, wrote to the current women's players to remind them this team is "not about the soccer"—that among the things she really misses most are "the weekly team devotionals ... the fellowship of a loving team and seeing my teammates' beautiful faces each and every day." Unusual perspective from an All-American.

From the opposite vantage point, that of a prospect with options, Kasiguran told the media in 2005: "My parents invested lots of money in my soccer career and I worked hard. They'd say 'This will pay for your school.' That was the goal."[13]

They reached that goal, too, with Kai receiving scholarship offers, including from the University of Akron, one of the top ten D1 teams in the nation. But then the Kasigurans changed plans, choosing Messiah. Why? "The most important thing for me," Kai told the campus magazine, "was growing spiritually and being prepared to be a man God could use ... I knew that could happen at Messiah and under Coach Brandt's leadership."[14]

And Brandt's take on Kai? "Other players of his caliber were playing 85 minutes a game; he was playing 55. But he was okay with that. He was a great fit."

For years the Messiah coaches have populated their rosters with "great fit" players like Kai and Kacie, ascribing to a have-it-all philosophy that's been around for a long time. Coaches and players alike refer to it by the shorthand "the genius of the and," a term popularized by business researchers Jim Collins and Jerry Porras in their mid-90s best-seller, *Built to Last*. In brief, the concept is the antithesis of what's called "the tyranny of the or," the presumption that there is a necessary tradeoff, that we must choose between seemingly competing ideals.

They want both. They insist on both. Usually, they get both.

Women's Coach Scott Frey puts it this way: "'The genius of the and' is taking those things that seem diametrically opposed and saying yes, we can have them both. I want the most loving, caring, relational girls I can find, *and* I want them to fight like crazy just as soon as they step across the line. I want both, not one or the other."

His recruiting packet makes clear to prospects the kind of paradoxical ideals this team holds in tension:

- A fiercely competitive spirit AND selfless love
- The hardest working team AND the most technical team
- Champions heart AND humble spirit
- Driven individuals AND selfless teammates
- Dare greatly AND the courage to fail
- Goal: to be a champion AND being a champion is not our purpose

USA Today perceptively added another to this list in a 2009 cover story, concluding "the secret to (the women's team) success is plain to see: Each wears a game face with joy on it." Game Face-Joy. Perhaps that's a future locker room ligature.

A recent note from a rival offers further evidence that "the genius of the and" is more than a slogan or aspiration. After a six-nil drubbing of nearby Dickenson College, a Dickenson player emailed Frey:

> "I just wanted to commend your team. I was extremely impressed with the women I played against tonight. I am not only referring to their undeniable skill, but also their sportsmanship on and off the field. Playing against them was an experience that I never have had. Not only were they gracious after defeating us, but they were the nicest girls I have had the pleasure of playing. You should be proud of the impression that they leave on their opponents. I wanted you to know how much I appreciate them...(They) are not only talented soccer players, but wonderful people...Good luck with the rest of your season!"

On the men's side, examples of their both-and character also abound, but one statistic may stand out as most telling. In the 2010 season, they not only won the National Championship but they did it while drawing the fewest yellow cards of any men's program in the nation at any level. A mere three cautions in 24 games. Maybe nice guys can finish first after all.

"The genius of the and" is taking those things that seem diametrically opposed and saying yes, we can have them both.

Scott Frey
Women's Coach

Now, in fairness, Coach McCarty says that because of their physical play, they probably deserved a few more cards, but this much is clear: Messiah recruits gifted kids who won't play soft but who won't play dirty or retaliate. "We want to be an extremely technical team and an extremely tough team," says Assistant Men's Coach Aaron Faro. "Many teams are tough but not great soccer players and many have great soccer players but they're not tough enough. We want to be both and there's no reason that we should have to choose."

So they don't. Nor did they, as we'll see later in this chapter, even before they could flash NCAA trophies to attract top prospects. But before we consider the specifics of their recruiting strategy, let's look at a second element of their recruiting philosophy: "critical mass."

A Critical Mass of Division I Athletes

Historically, the men's program had always attracted quality athletes, some of them All-Americans and some of them playing more than one sport. After all, Layton Shoemaker didn't win 72 percent of his games on sportsmanship. But when Dave Brandt took the helm in 1997, he sought to take recruiting to another level. As he tells it, in the late 1990s "we tightened up standards in every area: on the field, off the field, maturity, type of kid. On the field I was looking for a kid who fit our playing vision and off the field I valued a kid with a great heart and a high level of maturity. He was going to buy-in, work hard, be selfless, have no element of attitude or ego whatsoever."

In practical terms, that meant the goal of this Division III program was to lure away athletes from mid-major Division I programs—no small task since that requires recruits to give up scholarship money. But believing these kids were out there, Brandt's standards were both high and non-negotiable. It turned out to be exactly the right call: He and his staff attracted a bumper crop of extraordinary players in their first few recruiting classes—a primary reason the team won it all in 2000.

In fact, according to then-Assistant Coach Jason Spodnik, the 1999 recruiting class validated the coaches' perseverance and was the real breakthrough, with several D1-quality players joining the squad. In particular, he recalls: "There were many defining moments, but getting this class was at least in the top two, without me knowing what the other one would be. It was the right fit and the right guys with the right attitude, and it opened the gates for lots of things to come."

This is valuable perspective. Insisting on high standards to get that breakthrough class or breakthrough year can really get the flywheel turning, to borrow another Jim Collins metaphor. Winning it all creates an inflection point.

It's important to note, though, that finding a few special players to carry the team was never the strategy. Not in the late 90s and not today. Rather, *the primary strategy all along has been to attract enough of the best-fit players to move the culture forward.*

"I'm a great believer in critical mass," says a didactic Dave Brandt. "When you've got critical mass, outliers are just that. In the early 90s, we had less critical mass. We had pockets everywhere (of decent kids and not-so-great kids). And that's what changed. There was an intentionality right away to get more consistency."

He elaborated, making this essential point: "You don't want to burden the right people with the wrong people. Surround them with people of similar quality, people who will sharpen them."

Then, he says, the whole thing builds on itself. "Once you've got critical mass, it attracts. It pulls in more of the right kind of people."

In other words, success can beget success. The best athletes want to play for a winner. Recruiting gets a little easier every year. "It used to be that we went for Christian kids who lived in the region" Brandt told a reporter in 2005, reflecting on his nine years as head coach. "Now kids are contacting us (from all over) because we're good."[15]

Note the philosophical shift. It's instructive for any leader. Brandt insisted on pursuing "both-and" players for every spot on the roster, culminating in a "critical mass" of D1-quality athletes who also fit his attitudinal standards. This was pivotal. Consequently, they're now at a point where more than half the current men's team turned down D1 or D2 opportunities (and the scholarship money) to play for D3 Messiah.

The secret to (the women's team) success is plain to see: Each wears a game face with joy on it.

USA Today

Over in the women's program, they too have made the shift. Like the men's program, the women built a distinguished track record of attracting quality athletes before the breakthrough years, notching a 117-74-9 record from the program's inception in 1988 through 1999. But since Scott Frey took over in 2000, the stats have skyrocketed: A winning percentage of .927 through 2010. The change is highly correlated with the recruiting standards.

Frey's recruiting approach begins by simply telling it like it is, encouraging the best-fit players to self-select into the recruitment pool and the others to self-select out. His Web site puts it this way: "We seek to attract high-level players who have a passion for the game as well as a commitment to living by and embracing Christian principles in all that they do, on and off the field. The team's motto, 'One in heart and mind' (Acts 4:32), is a reminder of how we have been called to live as Christians. Each person willing to give of herself and her talents for the betterment of the entire group."[16]

Moreover, Frey also follows the philosophy of elevated standards and critical mass. "You always need special players and we've had them. But along the way, you need really good players all around them to make it work." Notwithstanding, he's still a bit somber reflecting on the upward shift: "A number of times I've said 'no' to wonderful young ladies who just weren't where they needed to be as a player. It was always the soccer piece of it, not the character piece because they're all so terrific."

Those hard conversations, though, have seemingly been the right conversations. Now, having reaped the rewards of raising the bar—a mere ten losses in the last ten years—his recruiting criteria are at an all-time high: "I know what I want to see. I want a girl who can play in the NCAA Championship."

How They Get Them: Messiah's Recruiting Strategy

There are some essential lessons in all of this for team-builders everywhere: Set the quality standard exceedingly high; prioritize character, insisting on a humble, team-first attitude; communicate these criteria unashamedly; don't settle for what you don't want; and achieve critical mass so teammates will sharpen one another. There is simply no substitute for having the right people, and contrary to what we might think, there may be no tradeoff involved in getting them.

But that begs the practical question: *how do they get them?* It's one thing to sit in a cloistered office and muse about raising the bar on recruiting to reach a new threshold of excellence; it's quite another to actually do it. How has Messiah found increasingly exceptional athletes, especially when they've narrowed the pool to their niche, Christian athletes with a selfless and coachable attitude? And beyond that, how have they persuaded them to forego the monetary and status rewards afforded by Division I suitors?

How They Find Them: An Exceptional Camp and Scouts Everywhere

Once upon a time, like many other programs, the men's team tried to develop players through a junior varsity program. According to Brandt, "We had been a full varsity and full JV up to Layton's last fall (1996). But the reality was that we were recruiting right over these JV kids. They weren't getting the gear or enough attention from the coaches. They got the leftovers of everything and were like second-class citizens. So JV wasn't creating a real pipeline for us. There were just too many guys to train."

Forty in all, between varsity and JV, and the resources just were not available to develop them. So Brandt's vision was to jettison JV.

An easy call, right? Not really, because the JV program had been there so long and frankly, in Brandt's words: "Who was I? I hadn't won a game yet (as a head coach). And we were successful in the 80s and 90s, depending on your definition, so this was a risk."

A risk he chose to take, consistent with his entire *modus operandi* coming in the door—one that, in the end, seemed to pay real dividends as it enabled the coaching staff to maintain a single focus.

We'll see the upshot of that in a minute, but if I may, there's another important leadership lesson here: *simplify*. If you're being spread too thinly, then focus your resources to do fewer things with more excellence. There's a second lesson as well, in particular for new leaders: *stand firm*. Be courageous and make the gutsy calls. There will be long-standing elements of your system that need to go—sacred cows that should be barbequed. Fire up the grill and grab your spatula. Make the necessary changes and move on.

Creating a Pipeline through Camps

So if not from JV, where would Messiah find these "both-and" players, these guys who had the skill to play D1 coupled with the humility to fit a team-first culture?

From two pathways in particular that ultimately became two super-highways: The summer camp and an expansive, energized alumni recruiting network. And in fact, there are no tolls on these highways, which fits the soccer budget nicely. The camps have made money and the alumni network is essentially cost-free.

The boys' summer camp has been around for decades, growing consistently under Shoemaker's shepherding. Basically it went from a little kid camp in the late 1970s with a van driving around to pick up the children, to a respectable middle school camp in the 1980s, to a high school camp that could rival what was traditionally considered the region's top camp, Elizabethtown College (the 1989 NCAA D3 men's champs). Shoemaker's enthusiasm and talented camp staff, led by Dave Brandt, in addition to Messiah soccer's escalating reputation, made the difference.

When Brandt put his own stamp on it as head coach in the late 1990s, it really took off. According to Greg Clippinger, standout center-mid from 1980-83 who has been involved in the camps since his undergraduate days, Brandt's focus on the Dutch system, his demand that campers work at a high rate, his teaching of more technical elements, and his adding a goalkeeper camp all combined to kick it up a notch. Brandt brought more into the curriculum and challenged the kids, essentially giving them a college-level experience as high-schoolers. The two-day "Advanced Camp" was a master-stroke innovation, attracting good-fit players to campus and giving those players a glimpse into the exciting future they'd enjoy on the men's team. That's now at 100 campers per year, with a waiting list. Complementing it is a day camp, a five-day resident camp and most recently, a team camp.

Coaches and other leaders take note: The drivers of camp growth have not been fun drills and low prices. They've been a high-level of training and a strong brand—and a *significant* investment of time on the part of the leader. Brandt, the former business major, just calls it like he sees it here: "Soccer coaches do an awful job with camps. I don't know what they're thinking—just rolling out the balls as a way to make money. It's glorified babysitting. I wanted everything that had our name on it—this is business and branding, of course—to be phenomenal, to exude excellence. So camps have been a big piece of the PR, the public image of our program. It was very important to me that if it said Messiah soccer, it was special."

Many of our recruits have come to camp since they were really small.
They sense from an early age the bond we have on the team and they want to be a part of it.

Bethany (Swanger) Sauer
Class of 2003, Women's Assistant Coach

Meanwhile, the same dynamics were at play on the women's side, which has emerged as one of the region's best camps under Scott Frey. 2003 grad Bethany (Swanger) Sauer, who has been working the camp since her undergrad days and who is now an Assistant Women's Coach, extols Frey's leadership here: "One of Coach's strengths is getting people to work together toward a common goal. He's done that in a lot of areas, including the summer camp," which, she adds, seems to get more effective every year.

As with the boys' camp, growth in the girls' camp has come from ratcheting up the standards and employing top Messiah players as camp coaches. Enrollment has grown more than 60 percent since 2001, Frey's first year as head coach, and now attracts more than 600 girls in a summer. Moreover, those girls are treated to a vision for what women's soccer can be, an eye-opening look at the level of commitment required to play for Messiah. Campers watch the current players working feverishly, whether they're demonstrating the drills or scrimmaging full-field. Also, knowing that your camp counselor sprinted twenty 200s with a mere 90 second break between them—at 5:30 in the morning—can be quite an epiphany.

The best players tend to get excited about challenges and these camps don't disappoint. Beyond that, they get to meet and eat with and play alongside current Messiah players, and even hang out with them in the dorms till late at night—a huge selling point for the camps.

It also motivates D1-caliber players to choose Messiah. Representative is Leah Sipe, an All-Region midfielder. "I was verbally committed to a Division I school and then I came to a Messiah soccer camp. There is just something special about this place that I felt nowhere else. I knew that I had to get out of my commitment and come to Messiah. Never once did I ever think I made a mistake."

Then there's Erin Hench, who went from elementary school camper to All-Everything forward and D3 National Player of the Year. "In 6th grade I began going to Messiah soccer camp. I looked up to the players so much. I even kept in touch for a while with my first camp coach and kept everything she gave me in a box with her name on it."

Years later, when Greg Clippinger, Erin's high school coach, was fielding calls from college scouts about Erin, her destination was still never in doubt. "I loved Messiah," she says, "and in 6th grade and I knew that's where I wanted to go to college."

That's not an anomaly, says Bethany (Swanger) Sauer. "Many of our recruits have come to camp since they were really small, both in-state and out-of-state ... They sense from an early age the bond we have on the team and they want to be part of it."

Scouts Everywhere: An Army of Mobilized Alumni

Greg Clippinger sent a lot of other players Messiah's way, too. For instance, in the late 1990s he contacted Brandt about Chris Boyles, "a diamond in the rough" who was not being heavily recruited. "He's quite an athlete who's always pushing himself," reported Greg. "He'd thrive in your demanding system."

Quite an athlete indeed. Not only did Boyles become an All-American goalkeeper for Messiah, he went on to win the NCAA Division III decathlon his senior year.

This is typical, part of Messiah's competitive advantage. "Everywhere you turn, there's an alum who can help the program get to the next level," claims Todd Suessmuth, a former player and current radio announcer for the men's soccer games. His comment may, in fact, be a bit of an understatement. At every turn there seem to be *two or three* soccer alums there—and they *eagerly* contribute to the success.

The reason is obvious, according to Coach McCarty: "When someone is happy with the product, they tell others about it." His Assistant Coach, Troy Sauer, agrees: "Alums will do anything for the program because of the lasting impact the program has had."

Simple reciprocity. And when it comes to recruiting help, the men's and women's programs may actually be reaping in excess of what they've sown. By one current player's estimate, between fifty and seventy-five percent of the current men's team found Messiah through an alum.

However, it's not just anyone the alumni are finding, and it's not just a recent phenomenon. Tim Houseal, a player from the 1980s, is a representative illustration of the advantage this creates for Messiah. Tim has personally recruited dozens of players over the decades, scouting out kids as early as middle school to get them on the Messiah radar. "Back in the 1980s," recalls Tim, "I watched an eighth grader named Brad McGlaughlin playing with the big boys (high-schoolers) and immediately saw the potential and let Messiah know. Eventually, Layton recruited him and Brad went on to become an All-American at Messiah."

Tim also helped broker the relationship between a young high school standout named Hayden Woodworth and Coach Brandt. Hayden was attending Tim's church and had started to play for a local team Tim was sponsoring. Long story short, Hayden ultimately passed on D1 Penn State for Messiah, becoming an All-American and even earning the D3 Player of the Year award.

A yawner of a story? Perhaps if it ended there. Fast forward from the recruitment to 2000 and the NCAA semi-final game. Things were looking grim as Messiah trailed two-nil at halftime, but then, as told by an effervescing Suessmuth, discernibly breaking into his accelerated radio announcer cadence: "Hayden singlehandedly carried us in the second half, scoring a goal, drawing a penalty, and setting up a third for a 3-2 Messiah win."

Not just any win, though. A win that propelled them to the championship game and Messiah soccer's first national title. Seven more would follow in the next ten years for the men. More than a couple program insiders cited that semifinal game as a turning point in the men's soccer program—a turning point made possible, in part, because of a committed alumnus looking to transform a program that transformed him.

Everywhere you turn, there's an alum who can help the program get to the next level.

Todd Suessmuth
Class of 1990

These are two of countless examples. Messiah has scouts everywhere—scouts who not only send information but who also sell the program—and it doesn't cost the College a dime.

Though to a lesser extent, it happens on the women's side as well, as Coach Frey explains: "We're not as old, so we don't have as much of a network. But our alumni network is still a great asset to have because they sift for us."

Sift is a good metaphor and a more challenging task at Messiah, since they insist on finding players that will fit their unique culture. Alumni know first-hand what that right-fit looks like and then they do the sifting, communicating important subtleties that are not always discernible from statistics or showcases. Reported one, "sure, the kid's a church-goer and says the right things, but he's really all about himself on the field—not defending, not getting back well, refusing to pass."

Thanks, we'll cross him off the list. We've got another 199 to consider anyway.

Beyond that, many of these alumni are themselves high school or club team coaches, running the same 4-3-3 system that Messiah does, so it's that much easier for them to identify kids who are a fit for Messiah's approach. As such, both the men's and the women's programs have for years benefitted from feeder schools in multiple states that regularly send the "both-and" players necessary to make the whole system work.

And they feel privileged to do so. "As alumni," remarks Suessmuth, "we always feel like we have the next sparkling recruit." Houseal takes it a step further: After a goal or a big save, alums sitting in the stands good-naturedly boast "that's my boy! I brought him in to the program!" almost as if the player were a son or younger brother. "This is a fraternity," Tim concludes, explaining the level of alumni commitment. "We want to see it continue the way it was when we were playing."

Standard Recruiting Practices As Well

Like other programs, Messiah coaches go to showcases to observe top high-school prospects. Like other programs, the coaches maintain an attractive recruiting Web site for prospects to learn about the program and to send their stats and videos. And like other programs, they extensively interview each prospect on the short list, as well as the family, to try to gauge the intangibles (though even here, Messiah may be a bit distinctive. McCarty, for example, says: "I also look at how a kid treats his mom, because moms say the darnedest things and embarrass their kids. Some kids are slumped over and give their moms dirty looks and some kids just sit there and smile and they can handle it." Not determinative, necessarily, but a piece of the puzzle).

The point is that indeed, Messiah engages in the standard practices to find and filter its prospects. Its real secrets to recruiting success, though, reside elsewhere; in particular, having a superior summer camp and a highly-motivated alumni network. Much like professional soccer organizations around the world, identifying promising prospects at an early age and developing them through a transformational youth program (in this case, camps and alumni-run high school teams) may give them a significant edge.

How They Persuade Them: A Unique Recruiting Visit

Still, why do D1 recruits give up scholarships to play for D3 Messiah? Why have they said no to places like Penn State, Notre Dame and even perennial powerhouse Akron for obscure Grantham, PA, a place so small that its post office still closes for a 60 minute lunch?

It would be easy to point to the championships and the greater likelihood of playing time in D3 as the answer. Next question.

Not so fast. There are two problems with that simplistic answer. First, Messiah is a relatively pricey private college and, as an NCAA Division III school, it offers no athletic scholarships. Consequently, the families of D1-caliber recruits pay a steep financial price—sometimes six-figures over the course of four years—for the privilege of playing soccer at Messiah. Second, both the men's and women's teams have been attracting this kind of talent since the days when they had as many national titles as nearby Keystone Technical Institute.

So there's been a lot more to the persuasion strategy than one might think. Which brings us back to the question of *why Messiah?*—a question that anyone in leadership must be able to answer cogently about his or her own team.

Part of the answer is that there's a lot to like about the College: a rigorous academic program delivered from a Christian worldview, the 13-to-1 student-faculty ratio, and a safe, sane environment. Another part of that answer, related to the soccer program, is summarized by Dave Brandt, sounding like an astute entrepreneur: "We try to create something of such value that they will pass up other opportunities to play in a higher division. All of our guys had cheaper options…to play at colleges where they would have received scholarships."[17]

But what often puts recruits over the top in both the men's and women's program—and this is part of the value proposition to which Brandt refers—is their visit to campus.

"We're very intentional when a girl comes onto our campus," says Coach Frey. "We're not just hoping they have a good time. There's a plan…so that when they visit they say: 'This is unbelievable! This doesn't happen on any other visit … These people really love each other, there is a commitment to excellence and a commitment to one another.' So that at least gives us a chance with the best recruits. And then you hope mom and dad foot the bill."

We're very intentional when a girl comes onto our campus. There's a plan so that when they visit they say: "This is unbelievable!"

Scott Frey
Women's Coach

It's a continuation of what we saw in the previous chapter. Frey and his team are assiduously intentional about this, attending to all the details, essentially choreographing the recruiting visit from beginning to end. 2011 captain Kelsey Gorman explains: "Coach picks who the recruit will stay with, based on personality or maybe because they're from the same area back home. Then, as a team we do what we'd do anyway—spend a lot of time together. We just include the recruit. But we also schedule some extra team activities when a recruit is here.

"Almost all of the recruits have D1 or D2 options," she continues, "so we have a team weekend with them. It's really helpful because it lets them see how close we really are and how well we get along. It also shows that Messiah is a different place."

The whole team getting together with a recruit may not seem like a big deal until one examines the reality of recruiting visits elsewhere. Often, prospects just hang out with a freshman or two, playing video games or tagging along as they go to a party. Occasionally, the upperclassmen stop by to subtly gauge whether you might take their spot.

It's especially true of men's soccer. "On one D1 recruiting visit," said Josh Wood, a standout player who came to Messiah from Tennessee, "one guy ditched me and another got a DUI. But at Messiah, even though freshmen house the recruit, we all do a lot of stuff together during the visit. The whole team cares that you're here."

The planning is meticulous, he says. "There are lots of meetings and emails about the recruits who are coming and what the schedule is. Particular players are also tasked with talking to the parents, riding with them to the dorm and that sort of thing."

It's all by design and it all matters if we want to get the best, says Wood. "People always come here with this D1 mindset. Some of them come to campus because of the championships, but what hooks them is the team. People are interested in you as a recruit and want to invest in you. Recruits play cards with us and go bowling with us and see that we love to be together. It's just different from D1 and D2 visits where people don't even want to know your name."

That sold 2010 captain Katie Hoffsmith as well: "During recruit weekend I fell in love with the girls—a big turning point. It was all fun and joking around. I thought, 'is this really college?' The girls were sweet. And there was no peer pressure or drinking. I didn't want to be involved in that at all." She chose Messiah, was eventually named to the All-Conference and All-Region teams, and anchored a bedrock defense for a class that was twice national champions and twice runners-up. Not a bad return for designing a recruit weekend for Katie.

The same was true for Katie's classmate, Amanda Naeher, who clearly could have played almost anywhere in the country. In an interview with CBS Sports, she too pointed to the culture of the team as pivotal: "There was something just a little bit different about Messiah than some of the other schools I looked at. I liked that it was a Christian school, I liked that it was a small school, people actually wanted to be here and be with each other. Everything is for the focus of the group and not the individual."

The tales continue about the disproportionate influence of the recruiting visit. Recall the story from the Purpose chapter (Discipline 1) about how All-American Troy Sauer was originally disposed against Messiah? The recruiting visit changed that. As Troy tells it, when he visited D1 and D2 schools, "The teams were good and the guys were okay, but when I came to Messiah, I just *loved the guys* and within 40 minutes I knew I was going to Messiah."

Recent recruit Sheldon Myers shares a similar story, albeit from more than a decade later: "I visited some D1 schools—Temple, UNC Charlotte, Bowling Green—and just hung out with freshmen. People just wanted to know how good you were and whether you might get money, all stuff that could relate to them. They didn't care much about me at all.

"At Messiah, Coach McCarty met with me and my parents. He talked about the importance of humility and team chemistry. Then, the whole team was outside of Coach's office to meet with me. We went out for wings and I talked a lot with Josh Wood. I was real impressed because he's a big-time player, not just anyone, and he seemed concerned about who I was and how this team was about so much more than soccer. At the end of the recruiting trip I was totally sold. The team chemistry was clearly there—everyone was friendly with everyone. I wanted to be a part of that."

Even though it was late in the process, the coaches didn't offer Sheldon a spot right away. They came to his house and wanted to get to know the family more. "Before they left my house," Sheldon says, "they made the offer and I accepted immediately."

And the financials? He's paying for a lot of this himself, so "it was hard to not take the money (from the D1 programs)." But then he echoed many of the families who send their kids to this College: "It came down to relying on God. If God wants me to be here, I'm going to trust him."

This all-hands-on-deck approach to recruiting, as we see, has transcended time and gender. It's often definitive, too, especially during the past dozen years or so as the coaches have actively managed and grown team chemistry—another innovation that's by design and the subject of our next chapter.

Talent Is Not Enough

There are obviously other approaches Messiah takes to persuade their talented recruits. For example, alumni not only identify and sift prospects, they meet with them and their families. Moreover, the program is now using a form of "gray-shirting," allowing high school seniors who have enough credits to enroll in the College a semester early (i.e., in the spring before their first soccer season) to get up to speed with the system and improve their game for freshman year. Messiah is also making offers like D1 schools do—not with money, but essentially with scarcity: "We have seven spots, five of them are filled. What do you want to do?" They've gotten to a point where they can just gently put it out there and the funnel begins to fill up with the right people.

Whoever said Christians can't be competitive?

Dave Brandt
Men's Coach, 1997-2008

It's been a long road to get the system in place, a system that's been instrumental to their continued success. But it's a road that any coach and almost any leader can travel beginning this very day. For Messiah, step one was the assumption that *talent is not enough*—a signature part of Layton Shoemaker's lasting legacy. And step two was the insistence on the highest standards of capability and character, an area where Brandt, Frey, and McCarty have truly excelled. There's been a paradigm shift to "both-and" players, a shift that Brandt's players remember him emphasizing repeatedly through the rhetorical question, "Whoever said Christians can't be competitive?"

One thing's for sure: It wasn't anyone who's played the Messiah teams in the last few decades.

Discipline 4

Cultivate Team Chemistry

How Close Relationships Create a Competitive Advantage

"5:22, 5:23, 5:24..." The Coach calls out the time as the first girls begin to cross the finish line. The second group of runners cheers on this first group, imploring them to hold nothing back, to run through the pain, to finish strong. Some even sprint with them the last hundred yards, despite the fact they're up next.

One girl collapses after the final stride. Two others finish with tears in their eyes. All of them have left everything on the track.

Welcome to Preseason, Day One—the grueling mile-run that every Messiah player has worked toward all summer.

"A mile?" you might be thinking. "What's the big deal? Anyone can run a mile, especially college kids." Perhaps, but most don't run it like this. The women's target is six minutes; the men's is five. And about three-quarters of the squad succeeds, with the others close behind. Some fall to the ground in exhaustion. Some vomit. But it's over.

Years removed from the ordeal, many of the alumni can rattle off their mile times the same way people remember their exact SAT scores. "Yup, I know 'em," one typical alumnus told me. "5:10, 5:09, 5:10 and 5:13. I never made it."

Still, those are pretty impressive numbers, especially since this was a reserve keeper. And a pretty impressive standard for the team as a whole. Most D3 coaches set the bar lower in preseason—usually a twelve-minute two mile run for men and a fourteen-minute two mile for the women.

But here's where it gets even more interesting. Rewind the tape a couple months. Like many programs, the Messiah players have an ambitious fitness regimen assigned during the summer. Unlike many programs, though, these kids tend to follow it faithfully, pushing themselves beyond their perceived limits, even when no one's watching. Just an athlete and an iPod, training alone, always mindful of those few fateful minutes coming in August.

Why do they work so hard over the summer? It's not because they're worried about being cut. Each will have a uniform in September regardless. It's not that they'll have to get up daily at six a.m. during preseason for supplemental runs with the others who missed the mark. They won't. And it's not even to win a starting spot, because the run doesn't determine that.

Rather, what's motivating Messiah players to persevere through these solitary, summertime workouts is that *they're not really alone*. They carry with them the voices and the faces and the aspirations of every one of their teammates.

2010 grad Trey Overholt, a defender who clocked in at a blazing 4:38 his senior year, explains: "In their minds, guys weren't putting in the extra work for themselves but for one another. If you don't make the five minute mile—the measure of what you did over the summer—there's no discipline, but it's sort of shameful. The cultural norm is to do your best for the team, so there's a stigma associated with not aspiring to the standard. You're not disciplined by the coaches; you're just an outlier for a day or two. It's a much bigger deal to the individual than to the group."

So they persevere, the men and women alike, intrinsically motivated by something bigger than themselves, each recognizing, as it says in their summer workout packet, "if you are comfortable, then you are not training."

Indeed, by that standard, each of these athletes is training daily.

Team Chemistry: Friends First, Soccer Players Second

It happens not just in the summer and not just on Day One, but on Day 21 and Day 41 and Day 91 throughout the season. And then it continues the rest of the year—through the "treadmill parties" in the winter, to the spring season when they take on D1 competition, into the following summer. Messiah soccer players, almost without exception, push themselves to and then beyond their limits, on the field and off, even at those times when they're seemingly accountable to no one.

This has been the case increasingly over the last fifteen years, though many in the program exemplified this quality much earlier. When Dave Brandt was an undergrad in the early 80s, for example, he would, according to then-teammate Greg Clippinger, "crank out a 4:35 mile, throw up, and just keep going. He was just a machine that way, a great competitor."

But the Dutch style of play that has been a staple since Brandt and Frey took over the teams—quick ball circulation, lots of width, defenders and holding midfielders overloading the attacking third—demands top fitness of *every* player on the field. They achieve that, in part, through their "both-and" recruiting strategy (i.e., finding athletes who are *both* technically skilled *and* disposed to drivenness, as we said in Discipline 3). The other secret of success, though, as Overholt indicated, is that everyone expends maximum effort because they want to do their very best for the team. Because of their close relationships. Because of the camaraderie.

Because of their *team chemistry*.

Now, that may be a bit of a tired metaphor these days. It seems to be used everywhere in sports, and often in soccer. When the French men's team, World Cup champions in 1998 and runner-up in 2006, self-destructed in World Cup 2010, not even making it out of the group stage, experts called it a team chemistry issue (some of the players did, after all, go on strike *during the tournament*, refusing to practice). Many said the same thing about the England team that year, a squad of superstars that found itself on a plane to Heathrow after round two, having suffered its worst defeat in World Cup history.

But despite its overuse, "team chemistry" probably still describes better than any other term the internal dynamics of the Messiah teams. Besides, it's how they talk about themselves and their advantage.

It's also how the National Soccer Coaches Association of America (NSCAA) talks about this intangible, disproportionately powerful asset. Here's their current definition.[18]

"Team chemistry is:

- the ability of the players to get along with one another, to work smoothly and unselfishly under the leadership of the coaching staff.
- each player's recognition of the specific role that he or she has in the team approach.
- mutual feelings of loyalty and empathy for one another.
- the ability of the players to anticipate one another's moves and to blend their efforts into the team pattern.
- a strong sense of team identity coupled with total commitment to the program and coaching staff."

That indeed captures it well. But at Messiah, the definition may be a bit less elaborate.

When asked "what's the best part of being a Messiah College athlete?" current midfielder Leah Sipe put it succinctly: "I have 24 best friends. We're growing in our faith together and every team member is going to be at my wedding."

I have 24 best friends. We're growing in our faith together and every team member is going to be at my wedding.

Leah Sipe
Class of 2012

Some of the All-Americans from the past decade emphasize the same thing. Leah's teammate Erin Hench suggested: "If we were a TV show, our relationships would be the main plot and our games the sub-plot, not the other way around." 2003 grad Mindy (Miller) Smith seems to agree: "Relationships are the foundation of a team. You can never invest too much care and time in a teammate." And 2004 grad Erin (Benedict) Bills adds: "I am hard pressed to think of a college memory that doesn't involve at least one of my teammates."

Five national championships among these four women and not a breath about it when asked for their fondest memories.

The way the guys (and sometimes the girls) put it is: "We're a collection of friends first and soccer players second." As with the women, that's more than platitude or propaganda. It's quite real, though it's a bit hard for prospective players to believe it.

Sheldon Myer, a D1-caliber player who chose Messiah, remembers being skeptical during his recruiting visit when Coach McCarty said the team was friends first and national champions after that. "It sounds like a sales pitch," recalls Sheldon. "It's not very believable, but it turns out to be reality."

Current center forward Josh Wood was even more blunt in his assessment: "As a recruit, you think that's the biggest crock you ever heard." But three years later, Josh is now among the most adamant apologists that in this program, relationships and team chemistry come first. Results then follow.

There's also a helpful chemistry between the men's and women's teams, a mutual-support system that encourages and sharpens both sides. When a reporter at the 2009 Final Four asked women's coach Scott Frey whether there was a friendly rivalry with the men's team, Frey cleverly responded: "I think it's just friendly. There's no rivalry."

All-American forward Amanda Naeher, seated next to her coach, elaborated: "To give you some perspective about the men's team, when we were leaving (for the game) today, they snuck around to the back entrance of the hotel and waited for us and were just cheering and getting us all revved up ... We both want each other to succeed."

Defender Katlyn Musser then bottom lined it: "We're each other's biggest fans."

Four Ways That Chemistry Gives Messiah an Advantage

This sort of chemistry is a longstanding tradition for Messiah soccer. But has it really helped them on the field?

Building relationships and being friends with everyone seems like a nice, "Christian" thing to do, but it's hardly a game-changer, right?

Not right. Actually, not even in the same stadium as right. The truth is that close relationships create more than a competitive advantage for these team, they create a *sustainable* competitive advantage—that is, one that other programs know about but cannot easily replicate.

There's a plethora of group dynamics research that testifies to this. Without question, the most effective teams are "cohesive" ones (the academic literature prefers the term cohesion to chemistry). Loyalty, commitment, morale, retention, confidence, *esprit de corps*—they all flow from cohesion, and consequently, so do better results. Moreover, cohesion turns out to be especially important when the team task requires a lot of interdependence (like relying on multiple team members to score goals) or a lot of efficiency (like moving the ball around as quickly as possible). A classic example is a rowing team; a close second is soccer.

By contrast, report the Ph.D.'s, where subgroups or cliques persist—a pervasive occurrence among college athletes who are not only categorized by how long they've been in school (i.e., freshman, sophomore, junior, senior) but also by their positions and by who's made the starting line-up—cohesion breaks down and the team tends to achieve suboptimal results.

Whether they've studied that literature or not, the Messiah coaches know it. And they live it, working overtime to maximize the cohesion and minimize the cliques, using labor-intensive but invaluable processes we'll consider in a minute. First, let's look at some of the many benefits they enjoy from their decades of making team chemistry a top priority.

Maximum Effort

Listen to a couple of Aarons who are currently on the men's coaching staff. As players, they fought the battles of the breakthrough years, capturing Messiah soccer's first NCAA titles. It's not surprising, then, that they use battle language when describing the value of team chemistry.

Aaron Faro, a 2003 grad, says: "I think the chemistry has everything to do with winning games. It makes a big difference in how you fight. When I walked onto the field with my best friends in life, it impacted how hard I worked." Aaron Schwartz, a 2002 grad, agrees, relating the inverse: "When you don't have strong relationships, you don't necessarily want to bleed for that guy."

Chemistry inspires. It motivates people to maximum effort.

The Messiah women are motivated in much the same way. Leah Sipe built on her "24 best friends" comment like this: "We play for each other. If you can't find the motivation from yourself, look at the girl next to you and know she is busting her butt for everyone … We do not want to let each other down, which goes back to being best friends. Friends don't want to disappoint each other."

Her current teammate, Corrine Wulf, adds: "Every girl on the team is a hard worker, but how much harder would you work for someone you love? The way we push each other is incredible; it's evident at every single practice. Success cannot come only from talent and individual work. It comes from a group of talented people coming together as a team, ready to work as hard as they can so they don't disappoint the girl next to them."

Notice, they're fighting *for* one another, rather than against one another to gain a starting position. They're working as hard as they can out of love for one another, rather than out of competition with one another. They're striving not to disappoint one another, rather than striving for stats or awards or personal glory.

Current men's captain Sam Woodworth recalls morphing to this mindset: "Before my freshman year, every time I went out to run it was just a battle. But the subsequent summers, it was about what I could do for the team, not how I felt—more of an accountability to my teammates. I had to work as hard as I could, knowing they were doing the same for me."

This is a veritable coach's dream. Self-motivation and self-governance are everywhere on these teams. As a result, the coaching staff can spend less time strategizing to inspire players and more time strategizing to defeat their next nationally-ranked opponent. Says Assistant Men's Coach Troy Sauer: "The team chemistry at Messiah has propelled us to a whole lot of success that teams with as much talent or more talent just don't have."

In many places, freshmen are hazed or excluded, but here it seemed like a family.

Hannah (Levesque) Leatherman
Class of 2006

Recruiting and Retaining the Best

Top performance, year after year, requires top talent. As we saw in Discipline 3, Messiah has increasingly attracted that talent through a sophisticated recruiting system that leans heavily on the prospect's campus visit. The team chemistry—the fun these players have with one another—is a pivotal persuader for recruits.

But great chemistry not only attracts talent, it also helps retain it. Quality players adorn the Messiah bench, foregoing opportunities to start at other schools. Rarely have these students transferred, though, largely because of the environment. Aaron Schwartz, from whom we just heard, was a brilliant keeper who was edged out for the starting spot by All-American classmate Chris Boyles. Faced with the prospect of never starting at Messiah, Schwartz nonetheless remained on the squad and, instead of being glum or resentful, took on the much-needed role of emotional leader. His attitude? "I'd rather sit on the bench at Messiah than start anywhere else."

Good thing he stayed, too. Boyles got injured their junior year and Schwartz capably replaced him between the sticks during much of their 2000 national championship run.

There are plenty of similar stories. Many years, Messiah's second string could itself be nationally ranked, but these men and women remain with the program because of, at least in part, the camaraderie and connectedness they feel. And the upshot? Bench strength that's become a legendary advantage in Division III.

Playoff Performance

That bench strength in turn gives them fresh, talented legs when the other team is dragging. At the press conference after the 2010 Championship, a reporter asked a great question: "How in the world has the Messiah men's team gone 8-0 in National Championship games?"

Keeper Jake Berry cited their physical conditioning. Playing two intense games in two days requires a fitness level that many teams just don't have. Midfielder Tom Renko cited their depth. Messiah's talented second team allows the first team to play only 60 minutes rather than 90 in the semifinals, giving them an advantage the following day (when they'll again play only 60).

Fitness and depth, as we've just seen, are derivatives of great chemistry. Coach McCarty, though, linked must-wins to chemistry even more directly. "The culture and environment of the program" is the real secret weapon in their ongoing success, he responded, especially in big games.

Perhaps that also explains some of the other inimitable statistics like the men's 42-3 record in the playoffs from 2000 to 2010, or how they became the first team in D3 history to go through the NCAA tournament without allowing a goal (in 2004), or their losing only 4 of 39 overtime games during these years. And although the women's team has not replicated the undefeated record in the finals, their playoff results are similarly impressive, having reached 9 of the last 10 Final Fours.

Leah Sipe shares the chemistry-related reason, expressing the sentiments of a generation of players: "None of us, and I mean none of us, *ever* want the season to end, which is certainly a factor in our success."

Strength through Encouragement

Freshmen year is a crucible for college students, and in particular for Messiah soccer players. Besides navigating challenging classes, long-distance relationships, and living with others, on the field they're encountering demanding new standards and struggling to learn an intricate, intense style of play. "In high school," says three-time national champion Nick Thompson about the freshmen, "these guys played a certain way and were good at it. Now they have *no idea* what to do. They're like a lost deer, not knowing where to go.

"But upperclassmen encourage them," assures Nick. "This will take some time. I got this and you'll get it too. Hang in there."

Hannah (Levesque) Leatherman, a two-time All-American and member of the first women's championship team in 2005, remembers it well: "In many places, freshmen are hazed or excluded, but here it seemed like a family. During freshman year, I was a bit of a head case—expecting to play my position and getting upset when Coach kept putting me on defense. What was with this guy? But at some point a junior, Emily Benson, pulled me aside and said: 'Listen, Coach doesn't play mind-games. You need to trust him. He knows what he's doing.'

"I had so much respect for her and I was so honored that she'd take the time to talk to me about this. It was a real turning point. The way the upperclassmen treat the freshmen and sophomores really helps to build a tight-knit team."

Those guys (pointing to Messiah bench) never yell at each other. All they do is encourage each other! All they do is help one another!

An opposing coach rebuking his team

Importantly, this habit of encouragement carries over to games. Hannah's teammate, 2006 All-American Savannah (Lehman) Stolzenburg, recalls sitting in the stands as an alum watching a women's game. "A Messiah player had skyrocketed a shot over the net and held her head in shame ... A teammate ran up behind her, as if her only desire in the world at that moment was to console ... I suddenly remembered the selfless camaraderie that is such an integral part of this amazing Falcon program. Putting others before yourself, lifting up teammates in times of need and encouraging even when you may not feel like it—this is what I saw fleshed out in a very practical way that Saturday afternoon."

And other teams notice it too, coveting the Messiah culture yet unable to copy it. Men's Assistant Troy Sauer remembers fixing divots on the field immediately after a home game against rival York College. "I was close enough to their bench to hear the York coach tell his team: 'You guys gotta get off each other! When somebody makes a mistake or doesn't get you the ball, don't yell at him. Those guys (pointing to Messiah bench) *never* yell at each other. All they do is encourage each other! All they do is help one another!"

...and win lots of games, thanks, in part, to their exceptional chemistry.

Six Ways that Messiah Cultivates Chemistry

"Team chemistry isn't something that we hope for," says Coach McCarty. "It's something that we work really hard at. It's not easy, it's not simple, and it doesn't just happen. We've got to fight, scratch and claw for kids to invest in one another's lives.

"It might be a little easier for the women," he continues as Coach Frey nods in agreement, "but it's not normal for guys to invest in one another's lives. That's not how we operate. We're more task-oriented."

Nowhere are the Messiah coaches more intentional than in the area of culture-building, developing healthy relationships and community. As McCarty said so well, "it doesn't just happen." His mentor, Dave Brandt puts it even more didactically: "Leaders don't realize that they can dictate the culture. We cross our fingers and hope things work out, instead of dictating a positive culture of success."

Scott Frey concurs, though disinclined to use the word "dictate." Rather, to him, it's simply a matter of diligence: "There are so many little things that have happened along the way that have created this culture. There isn't one thing ... It doesn't just happen. You've gotta keep pushing. You've gotta keep it going."

Again, the theme of intentionality (Discipline 2) in both the men's and women's program. "Team chemistry is a conscious effort," concludes McCarty. "In the end it helps us win."

Let's look at how they cultivate it.

"Forced Family Fun": The Mandate to Spend Time Together

Strong relationships—whether on a sports team or among co-workers or in a household or wherever—require time. There's no substitute for this; there are no shortcuts. Just ask anyone who's tried.

And, of course, chemistry becomes more difficult the larger the group gets. For a team of five people, 10 relationships need be nurtured for every member to be connected to every other member. For a team of 10, 45 relationships must be maintained. For a team of 25, like many college soccer squads, 300 relationships exist. Add in four coaches and you're now up to 406!

You can dust off your old statistics book if you want to check the math. But in this light, it's easy to see why chemistry "doesn't just happen."

It's also easy to see why so many coaches (and supervisors and other leaders) neglect this aspect of their job. It's a daunting challenge, one that can be enormously time consuming. Beyond that, some team members resist investing time this way, preferring to get back to their "real work." So who needs the hassle of managing relationships, especially for a seemingly uncertain payoff?

Well first, the payoff may not be that uncertain if the research and the abundant sports anecdotes are to be believed. And second, at Messiah, as you'll recall from Discipline 1, the payoff is not the purpose. It's the environment they're after—"a team of grace" and "the best place in the country to play soccer." So they make relationship-building a priority, regardless of whether it affects the scoreboard.

Beyond that, oftentimes it's anything but a hassle. "We do some scheduled things together," says Frey, "like we'll get together at the house once a month to have some fun, maybe compete or just hang out (most recently, they've started calling it "FREYday night"). We've done high ropes courses, things like that ... Women just love to get together. When you create a great environment, they love it. It's a social thing for them. So it's important and we orchestrate it."

Meanwhile, on the other side of town, the men's team is going "nerd bowling" (i.e., dress up like a nerd and meet at the bowling lanes) or playing cards or just hanging out as a large group. McCarty shrugs: "A lot of times I couldn't care less about what the guys are doing as long as they're doing it together."

Team chemistry isn't something that we hope for. It's something that we work really hard at. We've got to fight, scratch and claw for kids to invest in one another's lives.

Brad McCarty
Men's Coach

There are times, though, in particular on the men's team, when players would prefer not to spend a Friday or Saturday night with teammates. Hence the term "forced family fun" (or "FFF"). Yes it's fun and yes it's a family event, but yes, it's also forced upon them. "No" is not an option.

"It takes a special kind of a commitment," says current captain Sam Woodworth. "Coach's email will simply say this is what we're doing, you've got to be there and if you can't, come talk to me. Sometimes guys' girlfriends get a little frustrated with the amount of time the guys have to spend together."

Did Sam ever try to seek a special dispensation from the Coach? "I did once and he said, no, you can't go. So I called my parents and told them I couldn't come home. That's just the way it goes."

That may sound harsh, especially in a D3 program, but that's not the way most players hear it. "Without that insistence, we lose the accountability," says Sam. "I wouldn't want it any other way than how we have it now."

If that were not enough, the men's coaches also need to be proactive about managing their players' mindset during FFF time. Says Dave Brandt: "I often told them when a team event was coming up, 'You need to be careful how you're thinking about this. This is going to be a good team time together but there are lots of competing interest—a girlfriend, a nap, whatever."

That kind of attention to detail continues under McCarty. Says Brad: "We talk a lot about the attitude they're supposed to have when they're together ... Their attitude needs to be right. Any time they're together as a team, it may not be the best thing for them, but if that's the best thing for the team, then you need to buy-in."

And beyond all that, the coaches coordinate team-building service activities (Discipline 1) and plenty of FFF when the team's away overnight for a game (Discipline 6).

If it sounds like a lot of work, it is, especially for the men's coaches. But that's simply the way it's been done for years, claims McCarty: "Success isn't random for us."

"Mean No Offense, Take No Offense": Preserving Relationships

FFF may be the most important way that Messiah cultivates chemistry, but it is far from the only way. Another essential habit for both the men's and women's program is to be proactive about minimizing conflict.

Lots of things can damage relationships, from a rough tackle in practice, to gossip, to cliques, to mere non-verbals that communicate criticism. Some of these actions are intentionally malicious, some are not, and some are simply misunderstood. Regardless, they all threaten team chemistry.

Messiah addresses this threat through their principle of "mean no offense, take no offense." Teammates are to say nothing and do nothing that undermines one another, and on the receiving end, they're not to interpret comments or actions as personal attacks. The default assumption is that no one in this program does anything to harm or disparage anyone else—so don't do it and don't hear it that way.

And, like almost everything else, it's regulated pretty closely. According to Brandt, "there's not even to be a snicker at a teammate's expense." Moreover, according to Assistant Men's Coach Troy Sauer, if at practice a guy shows some body language that publicly implies frustration with a teammate, a coach pulls him aside and reminds him: "that's not how we react here."

There are other benefits besides relational preservation. 2011 captain Kelsey Gorman explains: "What happens at practice stays at practice. We're not each other's friends at practice, but as soon as we step off the field, that's the first thing we are.

"There are 24 great field players vying for a spot, so it's pretty cut-throat at times. But Coach talks about this all the time—'the genius of the and'—and tells us to really go at it. Compete with someone *and* at the same time don't take it personally."

On the next field over, the guys are also beating the daylights out of one another. Playing that hard all the time is one of the ways that they "link training to the match" (Discipline 5). But underlying it all is this simple principle, "mean no offense, take no offense." Without it, the whole system would be destabilized.

If we were a TV show, our relationships would be the main plot and our games the sub-plot, not the other way around.

Erin Hench
Class of 2012

"Don't Recruit Over Players": Preserving Family

Brandt leans forward at the interview table, clearly ready to make an important point: "A lot of coaches say 'it's my job to find somebody better than you; it's your job to keep your spot.' Ours was a different philosophy where we said this is a family—this is a group of people who are dependent on each other. We weren't going to cut people's legs out. So we made an early decision not to recruit over current players. In order to follow through on that, we would regularly say no to talented guys."

That may sound logical in the context of Messiah soccer, but it's actually a bit radical. In the soccer world, like in the business world, there's a war for talent. We win by getting the best. And we keep our people working hard through the implicit threat that somebody better might take their place.

That's anathema at Messiah. They spurn anything that undermines the environment or the "family." It's another outgrowth of having a higher purpose than winning. Ironically, though, it may help them win, as we said back in Discipline 1, since in this case it preserves their distinctive chemistry.

"We weren't going to take another kid just because he was decent or even worry about whether he'd be playing against us," insists Brandt. "We weren't going to cut one of our guys. The influence on the culture would be toxic."

Exactly. If his players were always worried about retaining their place on the team, then how can they have a strong, healthy relationship with one another or the coach?

Related to this, the coaches delegate much of the recruiting decision to the team. Says McCarty: "After a campus visit, I rely *a lot* on what my guys say about a recruit. 'Did you like this guy? Is he immature? Did he talk about himself the whole time?'"

2011 grad Kyle Fulks corroborated that. "Coach will say to us: 'Okay, you've seen these seven guys recently. Who are the best three and why?' The team has *very* significant input into who gets spots because Coach wants people who will fit."

And once they do have their new class—essentially replacements for the outgoing seniors—the relationship-building process begins immediately. Part of it is through a "recruit weekend," now a staple of so many programs across the country, allowing the future freshmen to come in and get acquainted with one another and the team. But at Messiah, it continues throughout the summer.

"It used to be through mail and email, but now it's Facebooking," says Scott Frey. "A lot of the new girls also come to our summer camp to work. So when they show up the first day of training camp, it's 'how have you been? how's life? we missed you!' rather than 'hi, my name is, and what's your name?' and wondering if this person's going to be on the team four days from now."

It makes a difference. Recalls Corinne Wulf, quite fondly: "It began the second I committed to the team as a senior in high school. My future teammates started sending me emails and Facebook messages telling me how excited they were I was on the team. I came into college with twenty-four new sisters who took me under their wings and loved me from the start."

"One-on-One Gets It Done": The Power of Peer Mentorship

"Many of us have accountability partners over the summer to make sure we're all keeping up with the training," reports Kelsey Gorman. It's part of the broader spirit of peer mentorship that pervades the program.

Historically the mentoring on the women's team has been ad hoc, informal, and player-driven, an arrangement that Scott Frey has encouraged but not required. He doesn't really have to insist, though. It's simply who these women are, the older helping the younger wherever they sense a need. In fact, they're now taking the system a step further: "The team is putting together a peer mentorship handbook" says Kelsey, its lead author.

Mentoring has long been a staple of development on the men's side as well, even though they may be generally less inclined than the women to nurture one another. Jason Spodnik, a former player and Assistant Coach under Shoemaker and Brandt from 1996 to 2000, recalls: "We often said 'one-on-one gets it done.'"

The number one piece of developing team chemistry is time. Everything else is a bumper sticker. The only way any of it works is time invested in people.

Jason Spodnik
Class of 1992, Assistant Men's Coach 1996-2000

The concept, if not the language, carries over to today. Coach McCarty is emphatic: "We tell our seniors 'you've gotta find that freshman and invest in him.'"And it happens often. Current player Josh Wood had a typical freshman experience. "The best friends I had on the team freshman year were two seniors—Josh Mull and Brett Faro. They weren't assigned to me or anything like that. They just mentored me. I must have had about 20 dinners with Josh Mull, who started taking me out after practice."

Not surprisingly, Wood, now a junior, has begun to take ownership over the process. "I want to emulate these guys because they had invested so much in me. Now I want to pay that forward to the younger guys."

What perpetuates these powerful mentoring arrangements, as Josh said, is reciprocity, paying it forward. At least that's part of it. Another reason is their worldview. For the women, this is what a "team of grace" does: they love God by loving one another. And for the men, Nick Thompson explained their impetus in a CBS Sports interview: "Our team verse for the last ten years has been 'As iron sharpens iron so one man sharpens another' (Proverbs 27:17) and that really applies every day, whether in a game or a practice, we're always sharpening each other and trying to make each other better."

And they do, on the field, off the field, during the school year, and over the summer. One-on-one gets that done.

"Standard-Bearers": Leadership Across the Whole Team

"We talk about not just standards, but standard-bearers as well—guys who push the envelope."

Coach McCarty is addressing an audience of more than 100 business people who want to tap into Messiah soccer's secrets of success. "You can't be a standard-bearer in every area, but you have to find someplace where you make an impact, where you make the program better than it was before."

To his right, Coach Frey follows-up: "I talk about leadership across the whole team. Each of you has something that you do well—fitness, the best miler, a goal scorer, relationships, academics. I usually won't say 'you're it,' but sometimes I do. The other day I told a girl she was a great team-dynamic person—an encourager, someone who can drop people notes every day to build them up."

Though he seldom uses the term standard-bearer, he boils it down to the same thing: "Just be good at what you're good at. Quit worrying about not being able to run the six minute mile and lead from your strengths."

Dave Brandt was a forerunner of this concept at Messiah, encouraging—sometimes even directing—players to find a niche role. His perspective on the subject is worth extended quotation:

> "I'm a great believer in the concept of guilt—you weren't punished (for missing the five minute mile standard), but what do you suffer? You suffer the weight of disappointment of your teammates, your coaches and the *legions* of Messiah players who have gone before you and made that five minute mile important. But I'll also say in reviewing the run that evening that some of you didn't make it and that means your teammates picked you up... and maybe you owe us. And you know from how we define ourselves that there are a thousand ways to make that up. Maybe it means just being an awesome kid on campus. Or maybe it means picking up a teammate through encouragement tomorrow or whenever. There are lots of ways to do this."

Bottom line: Do your best at everything, but be great at something that matters to this team. Model it for your teammates. Raise the bar for everyone. Take on a role. Be a standard-bearer.

Notice, sometimes the role specifically involves soccer, sometimes it doesn't. According to Jason Spodnik, back in 1999 when they brought in Hayden Woodworth (a "both-and" player we discussed in the previous chapter), Hayden had astronomical expectations of himself. "He really started the trend of going above and beyond," said Jason. "He'd often ask a coach to stay with him after practice and we even had to set some boundaries. He was pushing himself too hard.

"Hayden wasn't a flamboyant, charismatic leader," Spodnik clarifies. "He was a young freshman kid at the time." But he became a model, a standard-bearer for effort, and ultimately the 2002 D3 Player of the Year.

Contrast Hayden with his younger brother Sam. Sam concluded early in his Messiah career that, in his words, he "wasn't here to be the best player on the team. My role was a willingness to invest in each of the guys. I really value that. I want to know them on the field and off the field.

"If my goal was to be Hayden," Sam continues, "I'd never be fulfilled, never be satisfied. Yeah, it's difficult to think I'm a junior and I'm still not starting, but even here there's a joy for me. I'm a standard-bearer in the second group."

Leadership is not a title but an attitude.

Dave Brandt
Men's Coach, 1997-2008

What does any of this have to do with chemistry? Why does it matter if everyone has a role? Again, consider what happens in the absence of this approach. Without it, players tend to categorize themselves and each other one-dimensionally, based on performance. Ultimately, there's an in-group and an out-group, which curtails chemistry.

But with the standard-bearer concept in place, *everyone matters*. Everyone is affirmed as having a gift and an essential role. Consequently, players keep buying-in and keep working hard, no matter where they fall on the depth chart.

"I want them to quit hanging on to what they don't do well," says Frey about how this applies on the women's team. "It's about putting kids into their strengths" and showing them they belong and can contribute. Or, as Dave Brandt likes to say, "leadership is not a title but an attitude."

"Team Over Individual": It's Not About You

An individualistic mindset endangers team chemistry; a community mindset enables it. So the coaches assiduously keep this counter-cultural message before everyone: *it's not about you.*

Representative is the men's summer training material: "The summer workout is not about you. The 5 minute mile is not about you. Our upcoming season is not about you. This is about the team and what we can accomplish together."

"I was always preaching the importance of team over individual," recalls Coach Brandt. "We told them right up front as a freshman: 'There may be no decision in four years that is in your best interest. Get it through your head now—where we eat, what we do on Friday night, how we warm up—it may never be the way you want to do it, but that's not the issue.'"

What *is* the issue? It's their basic core value that "we support the team mission regardless of our circumstances." The team comes first. Always.

Everything we learn here emphasizes "team over individual" and putting others before ourselves.

Geoff Pezon
Class of 2011

The women's team culture is no different. One of their core values is that they'll have not just a willingness but "an eagerness to sacrifice personal interests or glory for the welfare of all." 2003 All-American Erin (Benedict) Bills, in an inspirational note to her former teammates, wrote: "When you become a Messiah Women's soccer player, you enter a world where you must work as hard as you can for the good of the team. The 'must' is not a coach-driven must; it's an inner motivation ... It also means rejoicing when a teammate is successful, even if you yourself are struggling. Sometimes it means spending time with a hurting teammate, when you really need to study. Regardless of the task at hand, it must be done for the sake of the team."

Here's a practical way that the coaches keep their players thinking in terms of team: They avoid highlighting players as special.

According to Brandt, there's a "complete ignorance of any individual honors." When All-American awards came their way, or All-Region or All-Conference, "we just didn't give it much credit ... Also, I tended not to nominate players for 'Conference Player of the Week' since nothing that happened for us ever happened because of one player. It created a culture for us ... The team learned to think and operate that way."

It's an intriguing philosophy, one that Brandt boils down to this: "I'm anti-separate. I don't like putting guys in different categories."

The same appears to be true for Scott Frey. "I'm not a big captain person," he admits. "I'm big on our upperclassmen being responsible and showing what it should look like." But with respect to the captains he does name, "I tell them they need to be the most servant-minded people on the team."

These kinds of "team over individual" practices, as well as others we'll see throughout the book, may seem like little things, but they facilitate the chemistry and unity and selflessness that are at the heart of The Messiah Method. And they manifest themselves in timely ways, too. Remember the story earlier of keeper Aaron Schwartz stepping in for injured first stringer Chris Boyles? As he recovered, Chris started thinking about red shirting a year and sought Aaron's advice. Aaron replied: "Our best chance to win is with you in the net."

"It was hard to say," recalls Aaron, "because I wanted to play, but this was the better thing."

Team over individual. It's a signature Messiah value, perhaps with some other valuable results. In a fitting epilogue to the story, Aaron humbly says: "Chris made a save in the National Championship game that I just would not have made."

The Middle of The Messiah Method

"As much as I loved teaching the game of soccer," Dave Brandt told a campus reporter in 2005 after earning his third ring, "I realized that our team's culture, our group dynamics, and our mission and purpose would all be much more important … than how well we passed the ball."[19]

Further experience has only solidified his resolve on this issue. When I asked Brandt in 2011 to sum up his best advice to leaders in a line or two, he pointedly insisted: "There is nothing more important—*nothing*—than organizational culture. It is everything and it can be amazing anywhere. And it is 100 percent under your control."

Scott Frey walks lockstep with Brandt in this regard: "Other teams have great players and they should be better than they are. They don't have the culture or the teamwork or the chemistry." And Brandt's protégé, Brad McCarty, adds: "There are going to be teams that may have better records or more talented players, especially at the Division I level, but we want to be the best place in the country to play soccer. And that's the culture and environment."

The lesson: Cultivate team chemistry. Build the "culture and environment" you really want. Make it a top priority. It supercharges everything.

There is nothing more important than organizational culture. And it is 100 percent under your control.

Dave Brandt
Men's Coach, 1997-2008

We'll say more in Disciplines 5, 6 and 7 about developing the right environment, but notice that "chemistry" is at the center of the seven disciplines in this book. That's because it's at the center of Messiah's competitive advantage. And not just any advantage, but their sustained advantage. As a cultural driver, it takes years and inordinate dedication on the part of leadership for anyone to replicate it.

Jason Spodnik, who in fact did go on to replicate this culture and its commensurate results at the high school level, says plainly to leaders what's required: "The number one piece of developing team chemistry is *time*. Everything else is a bumper sticker. The only way any of it works is time invested in people. Period. If it were easy, everyone would do it."

Messiah continues to make the investment. Any patient, determined coach can do the same. It's how good players become great teams.

Discipline 5

Link Training to the Match

What Everyone Knows but Few Can Do

Samba Futebol. The Messiah women's team has experienced it first-hand, travelling to Brazil three times for some friendlies. On their most recent visit in 2009, they played pro teams with names like Araraquara and FC Santos—good teams. *Very* good team. Santos, for example, was led by the coach of the Brazilian women's national team and, at the time, included a wizard named Marta, the top female soccer player in the world.

So the 2009 trip wasn't only educational because of the new and exciting culture, it was educational on the pitch as well. The girls saw 1v1 moves that they might have watched on YouTube or occasionally dabbled with in practice, but had never seen performed under game conditions. They encountered quickness, speed and technical ability unlike anything they had experienced before. They conceded some rocket goals from range, and they got beaten up a bit, too. The run of play was not only fast but physical—to the point where Coach Frey joked with his team: "The only thing friendly about these games is that they don't count."

But despite the opponents being long on skill and, perhaps, short on hospitality, the Messiah women had a lot of game in them, managing a couple of wins and holding their own against some of the highest caliber athletes in their sport. It was a respectable showing, with some Falcons, including battle-worn keeper Autumn Reilly, turning in the best performances of their lives.

What may be more interesting, though, was the reaction the team got from some of the Brazilian coaches who not only watched them play, but observed their practices. Recalls Todd Balsbaugh, long-time Assistant Coach for Messiah, those coaches "were struck by the connection between practice and the game. Many Brazilian players will do what they're supposed to do in practice, but then do their own thing in the game. Not us."

Frey nods about that. "Some of their coaches told us: 'Our players won't follow the way yours do.'" In fact, it was fascinating to some of the Brazilians that the American players trust their coaches this much.

Back in the states, other teams have been fascinated as well. Frey and Brandt, and now McCarty, get calls regularly about the design of their practices. They've found a way to do what every coach knows should be done, but only the best ones are able to achieve: They train in a way that genuinely makes a difference in games.

Standardizing Soccer

As of 1997, team chemistry and great relationships had won the Messiah teams exactly zero national championships. Not to downplay the pivotal importance of chemistry, but the reality is that it's a necessary but not sufficient condition for success. The same is true of talented players: you need them, of course, but the most talented teams are not always the victors. It's true of expert coaching as well. There are plenty who are phenomenal but ringless. It's in fact true of every element of The Messiah Method. This is a system that produces optimal results only when all of the pieces are working together.

In the spring of 1997, what incoming head coach Dave Brandt needed was another piece of that system—a missing link, if you will: The elusive link between what happens in practice and what happens in the game.

Freedom becomes chaos without structure.

Scott Frey
Women's Coach

There's a reason it's elusive in soccer. This is arguably the most unstructured of team sports. Soccer, as it's typically played, is not like basketball or hockey or American football where offenses run designed plays that they've practiced a thousand times and where teammates' moves are predictable. And it's not like baseball which requires far less interdependence among teammates. In soccer there are eleven players on a side, each of whom has a dozen options with the ball and even more without it. It can be the Wild West of team competition, anarchy until someone brings order to it.

Dave Brandt, the new sheriff in town, was the right man for the job. Brandt imposed a logic and a tidiness on Messiah's system of play—a specific methodology by which the ball would reliably move from one place to another and ultimately into the net. Borrowing heavily from the Dutch, Brandt standardized Messiah's approach to the game, *thereby enabling them to train in a way that made a real difference in the match*. Here's the backstory.

Building the System

The Messiah men had been using pieces of the Dutch system for a long time. According to Mike Russ, a Messiah player, a men's assistant coach in the 1980s, and the head women's coach from 1989 to 1996: "Although Layton (Shoemaker) never called it the Dutch system, it had some of those elements. He focused on passing and moving the ball around quickly, speed of play, keeping possession, and changing the point of attack. But when Davey took over he specifically said we're going to play Dutch and created a complete system."

As Brandt tells it, in March of '97, soon after he was tapped to be head coach, Messiah was playing in an indoor tournament at Penn State. "Driving out of the campus when it was over," he recalls, "the Dutch 4-3-3 flashed in front of me—the positions, the little dots, all of it. I had seen it somewhere before in the last few months, but it just came to me in that moment. I said to myself, 'When I get home I'm going to start researching it.'"

He poured himself into the task, beginning with benchmarking. As far as Brandt was concerned, Ajax, the Dutch professional club managed through the 1990s by the renowned coach Louis Van Gaal, was the model. Van Gaal had led the club to national and European titles through a distinctive system of play.

"At the time," remembers Brandt, "Ajax was in the Champions League and on ESPN, so I taped a couple games and then broke them apart."

Dissected may be a better way of thinking about it. Or autopsied. At the atomic level.

Brandt studied everything the team did—every passing option they exercised, every run they made, every decision of every player—and began the process of creating a Messiah version. "It was possible," he says, because "the Dutch system was fairly mathematical. It would have been harder to do this with the Brazilian or Italian or Spanish game. They're more free-flowing."

Then Brandt studied some more, devouring books on the Dutch system, analyzing more video, even boarding a plane to see it for himself.

"The first trip we took as a team," says then-Assistant Coach Jason Spodnik, citing the summer of 1998, "was to Holland to dive into the culture and to learn as much as we could." Van Gaal, who had by then taken the top job at Barcelona, was now blending the Spanish style of on-ball creativity with the structured, robotic approach of the Dutch. So what Brandt and Spodnik ultimately converged on was, essentially, one part Barcelona, two parts Ajax. It added up to three years of experimentation and then breakthrough: their first national title.

"It started with more than sketches on a napkin," explains Spodnik about how this exciting time unfolded. "It was yellow legal pads full of ideas."

And phone conversations even more burgeoning than that, according to Brandt: "During the first three years we would talk on the phone an average of 90 minutes every night—solving problems, hashing it out, making decisions—essentially laying the groundwork not only for program philosophy, but for how that philosophy would be applied. I feel in some ways that I couldn't have done it without Spod."

In the end, all that work culminated in a standardized system, one that broke down the game into almost every conceivable situation and then dictated the options a player has in each of those situations. Like the Dutch, they'd play a 4-3-3 formation, using a flat back four, a triangle in the midfield (one attacking midfielder and two holding midfielders), a target man up top and two pacey wingers with white paint on their boots from playing so wide. For each position, they specified what their movements and qualities should be, parameters that are detailed in the Appendix to this chapter.

The coaches dictated a lot more than that, though. Specifying positions and qualities and tendencies is essential, but without more, there's far too much room for player sovereignty, the antithesis of standardized soccer. There needs to be something more to bring order out of chaos, alignment out of autonomy. And there needs to be a way to avoid the problem lamented by the Brazilian coaches, players who do what the coach wants in practice but then do whatever they want in the game.

At Messiah they found that way. It's called "team agreements."

Team Agreements

The concept was in place earlier, but Brandt got the actual term from a Dutch coaching school in 2001. Essentially it boils down to this, as Brandt represented it when speaking to hundreds of coaches at an NSCAA seminar: "Team agreements are things that the players must do or things that the players must do in a certain way ... It's not a choice. We agree it's what's going to happen."

Softer than a "rule," which carries a dogmatic connotation, "team agreements," claims Brandt, carry the connotation of collective purpose. They're "oriented toward a vision of who we are," leveraging social influence rather than authoritarian influence. They're at the same time less heavy-handed than "rules" and more effective.

And at Messiah, there are dozens of them, maybe hundreds. The chapter Appendix reproduces those agreements that are included in the men's recruiting packet, but here are a few top-of-mind examples as shared by some of the men's and women's players:

- Receive the ball across your body whenever that's possible
- Turn as much as possible to break pressure, rather than taking the easy way out and playing the way you're facing
- Always finish a cross with your front foot (the foot closer to the ball). The defender has more chance to poke it away if you take it with the back foot
- Be balanced when you make a pass or take a shot
- If you're off balance and can't take a hard shot low, then make another choice
- When a winger takes the ball across his body in the middle third of the field, the target needs to get out of the middle
- Penetrate on the ground through the seams
- When playing the wing deep, bend the ball inbound to the corner flag
- If a wing's option closes off at the end line, the ball goes back to the outside defender and then over to the other wing

Beyond the specifics of technique, there are also team agreements for relationships and culture and mindset. For example, one agreement, says Brandt, was that "we were going to think and act in a certain way. We were going to be open to doing what was best for the team rather than what was best for me. This was a big, big thing." Team chemistry. Team over individual. We've been down these roads earlier in this book and we know where they lead.

And what if you don't agree? What if you like playing long balls in the air because you had a lot of success with that in high school? What if you prefer to spend time with your video game controller rather than with your teammates on Friday night? In both the men's and women's program, that will get you a trip to the coach's office and then maybe to the far end of the bench. As Brandt makes clear: "It's not a choice." But as we just saw in Discipline 4, the real incentive to comply is that almost everyone believes this is what's best for the team. Says 2010 grad Trey Overholt: "From the sideline, if we see a player violate one of those options, we wince. Everybody knows what everybody else is supposed to be doing."

Team agreements are things that the players must do. It's not a choice. We agree it's what's going to happen.

Dave Brandt
Men's Coach, 1997-2008

Having said all this, there's still an important caveat, one that permits Messiah to tap the collective experience and creativity of its players. If on the field you have another option that works well, you can use it. But it has to work pretty often. Otherwise, you stick to the original agreement.

Assistant Men's Coach Troy Sauer likes to call this "freedom within a framework." Says Troy, a creative winger and All-Region selection himself in the early 2000s: "Guys do have some latitude to do other things, if you have the talent to do that. We need to be unpredictable and dynamic. We can't be robots, especially since teams scout us so much. We need to be strategic and think through what the other side is going to do and how we can be dynamic enough to beat it."

Over the years, a number of innovative and talented players have added to the repertoire of team agreements this way, creating, for instance, a fourth option in a situation when there used to be only three. To cite just one example, after a hard switch to the wing, the weak side holding midfielder (the 6 or 8 in their formation) can make a run into the box, giving the winger the option to play him. Those types of additions have really enhanced the system over the years and even carry forward the name of the person who invented them (the men, for example, call this a "Mohney Run," after its originator, 2006 grad Bryan Mohney).

"Freedom within a framework," of course, extends to the coaching staff as well. They've not just slavishly adopted the Dutch approach. Troy explains, revering his former coach: "So many of these team agreements came from a Dutch influence—from the coaches and books. But Dave definitely made those things his own. He has such a high understanding of the game and the intricacies that he can customize it."

Brandt confirms the customization. "I began to copy," he recalls, talking about Van Gaal's system, "but then you run into your own problems and have to adapt and solve them."

Indeed they have, building a standardized system and securing buy-in through team agreements. In doing so, they've made it more possible to link training to the match. Let's look next at how that training works.

Training Linked to the Match

Imported from Holland, the concepts eventually made their way to both Scott Frey and Brad McCarty. Specifying player options is fundamental to these coaches' systems as well. "Freedom becomes chaos without structure," Frey clarifies, almost proverbially. "Most soccer teams in the final third are hoping something good happens, hoping they score. We don't hope; we have a plan." McCarty is also quotable here: "If you're doing something in practice that doesn't show up in the game, you're wasting everybody's time. Most coaches haven't developed a system where positional play is so dictated, so they can't train as well for what's going to happen in the match."

To get a closer look at that training, let's take a seat on the bleachers at the Messiah practice fields. To the left are the men, to the right, the women. Some days they almost seem like mirror images.

Some Drills for Technical and Tactical Training

One thing we'll notice is that Messiah practices are surprising short, considering the complexity of their system and caliber of their competition—about 90 to 105 minutes a day during the regular season. But every one of those minutes counts, explains Frey: "We're right to the point, very intentional going from one drill to the next. Get it right and move on."

The practices are focused as well, as we said in Discipline 2. Frey continues: "Many coaches do too many things in one practice. Or they try to focus on a few things but they don't stay with that—like when they say they want the team to work on possession but then at the end of the drill they're mad about the team's finishing. I don't have every practice down to the minute like (UCLA Coach John) Wooden did, but we'll have only three or four different things we're going to do in a given practice. Actually, four would be a lot."

What do they do? Drills and games that are inextricably linked to their Dutch style of play. They didn't have to invent them. The Dutch had been road-testing and perfecting these for decades. From the days of Brandt and Spodnik to today, they've borrowed liberally from Holland, teaching off of platforms with names like "Dutch Diamond," "Dutch Square" and "Magic Diamond," and grafting in a host of small-sided games to develop specific technical abilities.

If you're doing something in practice that doesn't show up in the game, you're wasting everybody's time.

Brad McCarty
Men's Coach

They also sharpen tactical decision making through exercises like "shadow," a 10v0 game where the team plays against no defenders to practice pre-determined passing sequences that lead to scoring chances. Coaches can then incrementally add defenders to train these passing patterns under more realistic conditions. Frey points to it as a staple: "We play a good bit of 10v8 to do this under pressure. I can control the success factor (of the drill) based on having the right numbers (on defense)."

Overall, Messiah does not use a wide variety of drills. Instead, they tend to rely on a scalable set of exercises, starting with fundamentals, progressively adding new elements, and working them to perfection. Even today, Brandt says: "My collection of drills or exercises wouldn't be that thick of a book. We have things that are purposeful and relate and that work. People are shocked that there's not that much to it."

Repetition. It's long been a keystone for Messiah soccer because, as Brandt says, it works. All-American Nick Thompson lived it for years. "I felt a big jump in my personal game the first two years," claims Nick. "Repeating so many things really helped—doing the little things over and over again. It just becomes innate. Then in a game, you already know what you're going to do when you get the ball."

We'll look more closely at the value of repetition in Discipline 7. For now, suffice it to say that the drills' main objectives are as straightforward as they are ubiquitous: to perfect technique. Internalize the options that each player has in every situation. Repeat it enough so athletes can execute consistently under game conditions.

Messiah does a lot of tools training as well—Cruyffs and Dutch turns and 1v1 moves and the like—as well as training for specific functions that are clearly linked to the match. Says McCarty along these lines: "We don't do anything without a purpose in practice. Everything we do in practice translates to the game. Everything is functional, so if you're a right back, you're spending time on what you need to do. Now, there are times when it's general ... but overall, we work really hard to make sure that how we train shows up during a game."

So as one winger told me, after botching a cross in a game he spent half the next practice taking a few quick dribbles to the end line and then bending the ball in to the twelve. That's what he needed, that's what he worked on—100 times the next day.

Meanwhile, the head coaches are talking to the players non-stop. Teaching, actually. Reinforcing the linkages to the match. And they're *very* good at it.

Reinforcing the Linkage

Great leaders must be great teachers. Otherwise, few are influenced. Few follow. Skeptical? See how many you can name who are one but not the other.

Throughout the history of the men's and women's soccer program, Messiah has been blessed this way. And in the case of Brandt and Frey, their teaching ability is truly distinctive. Anyone within a quarter mile of the practice field can hear them, their incessant encouragement, their astute corrections, their exclamations and howls and cheers.

"Hit that with the other foot. That's too long a touch. Yes! That's what we want to see. Come on girls, pick up the pace. Don't let him turn on you like that! Step harder!"

They seldom let up, constantly educating, persistently perfecting, reinforcing the team agreements until they're second nature and first rate. It requires energy beyond what many coaches are willing to spend, but pays dividends beyond what many coaches will ever earn.

How is it heard by players? As it's intended, at least eventually.

Midfielder Sheldon Myer offered this comment at the end of his freshman season: "After awhile, the constructive criticism is heard as encouragement and teaching. As a freshman you're not used to this and it's tough trying to respond to the barks. There's lots of worrying about getting yelled at. Then you learn that you don't get yelled at if you do the right thing but shank it. You *do* get yelled at if you do the wrong thing and crank it into the back of the net! And after a couple months, it gets to a point where Coach says it so much that you just know what to do."

You need a textbook for all the terms and runs and options. Soccer is free-flowing but Messiah has made every position a set of options.

Josh Wood
Class of 2013

Importantly, there's also a significant element of *self-teaching* in the practices. Players teach and encourage one another, but more privately, and more pervasively, they're thinking to themselves about how the drill connects to the game.

Target man Josh Wood explained during our interview. Stepping up to the white board in my office, he drew two diamonds connected at one point, a standard drill they use to develop touch and speed of play. But there's so much more happening than that. It's a decision-making drill as well.

"If I'm here," Josh points to the top of a diamond, "I know that these two guys on my right and left are my sixes and eights and the guy across from me is my center back, whom I'd never play. So when I receive the ball in this drill, I never split it across the diamond since I'd never do that in a game. But if I'm here and I'm a holding midfielder," he continues, pointing to the same place, "I can play the split. Guys who play that position have more options in this drill."

It's hard to put a value on that cognitive habit. The linkage between training and the match is being reinforced in practice on almost every touch. As a result, when they're under pressure in game conditions, it's natural to make better choices which can then culminate in a scoring opportunity rather than a lost possession. Little things, as we said in Discipline 2, become big things.

Intensely Competitive Practices

"Practice the way you play."

It's a common, almost clichéd expression in soccer—a universal reminder to train at game intensity. In the Messiah program, though, they take a step further. 2011 senior Leah Sipe contends that "more times than not, our practices are *harder* than our games."

On the men's side, Josh Wood agrees: "As hard as I've been hit in a game, I've been hit harder in practice. And I've been more ticked off in practice than I ever have been in the game. When I was a freshman, Brett Faro almost broke my nose in practice with his forearm and he just went on like nothing happened. I wondered 'how could someone who's my friend do that to me?' But I eventually realized that practices are going to be harder than the games. This is the level of competitiveness that's expected all the time. We're not friends on the practice field. We go at each other."

Josh's bottom line is this: "If you leave practice feeling like it's been a practice and not a game, then there's a problem."

The intensity is at the behest of the coaches, of course, but it's also, Leah says, "because we're so competitive … which is great because we make each other better."

How competitive? 1990 grad Todd Suessmuth travelled with the men's team to South America in 2011 and has an answer: "These kids are as competitive as they come. They don't even like to lose a game of checkers. They were getting upset about losing pick-up games in the side fields in Columbia."

Apparently the trait doesn't dissipate after graduation, either. Todd continues: "The alums hate to lose when they come back for the annual game against the current team. There are emails flying around for weeks saying how we're going to win."

Notice in all this, again, the clear linkage between training and match play. Teams try to get rough with Messiah to throw them off their game, but they can't. Speaking for both the men's and women's team, Josh maintains that "nothing shakes us because we've been through it in practice." Plus, they've been trained repeatedly in practice to not retaliate or show frustration (recall from Discipline 4 the principle of "mean no offense, take no offense"). So they don't do dumb stuff that draws fouls and cards and hurts the team. They just stay on their game.

It seems to distinguish them in the post season as well, Josh claims: "Every other team at the Final Four is playing soccer horseshoes, trying to hit a cone with a pass, just happy to be there. They're going lightly with most stuff. But we run a regular practice, going at each other as cut-throat as can be. At the 2008 Final Four, Coach Brandt even had to stop people from going so hard at practice because he was concerned somebody was going to get hurt."

Practice the way you play? Messiah ups the ante: Practice harder than you play.

Training for Mental Toughness

"The psychological dimension has always been big with me," reveals Coach Brandt, commenting on how technical and tactical training is not enough. "Mental strength in athletics is everything."

Coaches transcending sports and transcending time have sung the same tune. Coach Frey and McCarty add their voices to the chorus as well. Frey tells his girls it's a choice. "Do I give in? Do I fight through it? That's a mental toughness issue. We talk about fighting through it—*choosing* to fight through it—all the time because you've got to do what's best for the team."

McCarty sounds much the same: "Mental toughness for me is your ability to focus on what you can control. If you start focusing on things you can't control, you're just soft because you can't handle your world around you, so you start lashing out at things that take away the focus. You've got to be able to handle when you get fouled from behind. You've got to be able to handle when an official makes a bad call."

And you've got to handle other tough situations as well, like when you want to stop training, but know you should push yourself further. Or when you're deadlocked in overtime with heavy, cramping legs, but you need to find that golden goal. Or when you're about to take a PK. Or when everything's on the line in a winner-take-all post-season match. Or any other time that fear or pain or fatigue or your emotions could keep you from your potential. The psychological part of the game is an issue of inner excellence, of resiliency, of bringing your "A game" regardless of circumstances. It's an issue of rejecting the pernicious self-talk that says you can't succeed; an issue of setting aside your feelings to do what's necessary and right.

Ultimately, it's an issue of competitive advantage.

The advantage is significant, too. Mentally-tough players and teams push beyond their perceived limits. After four years' experience with this, keeper Kyle Fulks had learned that "you can always push your body farther than you think you can. We're not going to settle for how we used to be. Our physical and mental potential is so much greater than we think."

The women learn the same lesson first-hand. “Some of them in practice,” Coach Frey says with an empathetic shake of the head, “will be running like crazy with tears in their eyes because they don’t want to give in.”

The psychological dimension has always been big with me. Mental strength in athletics is everything.

Dave Brandt
Men’s Coach, 1997-2008

Another advantage is that mentally-tough teams “finish strong.” Messiah’s stellar record in overtime games bears stark testimony to this, as we’ve seen in other chapters. The men also have a noteworthy record of getting game winning goals after the seventieth minute of regulation: Twenty times since 2000 they’ve done this; only five times have they given up a game winner in regulation after the seventieth minute. More recently, over the past three years, they’ve also been good at drawing level late in the match, finding an equalizer after the seventieth minute in eight games versus having yielded a late equalizer only twice.

Is that just outstanding fitness coming through? Or special players who have a knack for heroics under pressure? Part of it, no doubt, but often the competition has similar attributes. Rather, for both the men and the women, it’s also connected to the psychology of the game. Messiah usually pulls it out late because of the poise and determination that comes from mental toughness.

How to Become Mentally Tough

The question, then, becomes *is this trainable?* The coaches are unequivocal, having cultivated the attribute for years. Brandt's words exude confidence born of experience: "You don't have to lose to become mentally tough. ... We can dictate and train this."

For the men's team it starts with a phrase whose simplicity belies its power: "We separate act from feel." Distinguish these two things. Set them apart, one from another. Do what you're *supposed* to do regardless of what you *want* to do.

And although the women have not used that particular phrase (that kind of bifurcation does sound more like a guy thing, after all), the concept shows up in no fewer than three of the team's ten core values: "We choose to be positive ... Success is giving your best at all times, no matter the circumstances ... We do the right things for the right reasons, all the time" (which is, in fact, a throwback line to the days of Layton Shoemaker).

The point is that these teams have created a common and energizing language to keep the issue top of mind and universally understood. It's memorable and it resonates. Then, they make a priority of communicating the principle often.

Frey elaborates from his vantage point. "For guys, you can says 'suck it up, be a guy.' For girls, it's just different. Helping them foresee that this is going to be hard, and what will you do when that happens, and you can't sulk about this ...In these situations, we often talk about choosing to be positive, which is part of mental toughness."

The common language on the men's side—"separate act from feel"—has for years rolled off the tongue of most players. They're taught it early (some of the freshmen are most in need of this revolutionary reframing) and they're taught it often. Assistant Men's Coach Troy Sauer indicates, like Frey, the pivotal role of straight communication, as well as chemistry, to teach this challenging perspective: "Some players have difficulty separating their actions from their feelings, but if relationships are strong, you can talk about that. Corrective conversations are more available."

Modeling by the leadership and by the upperclassmen also makes a difference. Brandt goes so far as to claim that it "might be the most important trait for a leader ... Leaders can't afford to act out their feelings, at least in most cases." And they don't at Messiah. If you saw one of their soccer coaches berating a ref or losing it in the halftime huddle, it would be considered a rare sighting indeed.

The same is true for the student leaders on the teams. They walk the talk, or in some cases, run it. One of Brandt's classic approaches for training mental toughness is what he called "Messiah sprints." The Coach would, without being explicit about it, give players a chance to demonstrate for one another what it really means to "separate act from feel." He'd pick two or three players to run a few sprints at maximum effort while the whole team looked on. Then he asked those guys to join the team as they all ran the full complement of the sprints together.

Brandt would always pick the captains or the oldest or best players for this unusual role—guys who knew the system and what his rationale might be for the seeming unequal treatment. Their role was to model the principle of separating act from feel, and they considered it an honor. Plus they did it really well—they were right back on the line with an eager face to do their best.

Brandt's recollection? "It was amazing the effect it had on the team." Guys saw through their peers that it's possible to make the separation. They saw that people do not have to be a slave to their feelings or their fatigue, but instead, that a person could choose to persevere.

It all became even more real when each athlete began to experience *for themselves* the next level of mental toughness. Both the men's and the women's team accomplish this through "treadmill parties" during the off-season.

Frey explains: "I'm in their ear almost every day with an email about mental toughness. But we're also doing some training stuff on the treadmills that's stretching them and creating mental toughness. Friday is a 'challenge day'—go at a certain pace as long as you can (currently, it's 7.5 mph, adding 0.1 every minute until you can't continue.) What's a good time? I have no idea. You go as long as you can." And, he says, some girls figure it out pretty quickly, sheepishly admitting: "Coach, I'm not mentally tough."

"I know," he responds gently but with a chuckle. "That's why we're doing this."

The men's team has a longstanding tradition here as well: Set the treadmill at 11.2 mph and run for as long as you can, trying to reach two miles.

I'll save you the math: It works out to about a 5:21 mile. Two of them. Back to back. Pass the Gatorade … and the oxygen tank.

Why 11.2? Like so many Messiah innovations, this was Brandt's idea: "I did a lot of treadmill running myself at the time and I was pretty tuned-in to the right paces for our guys to train. 11.0 would have been too slow and 11.5 too fast for what I wanted."

So 11.2 it was and it remains that way to this day. Here's the key, though—and if you've read this far in the book, you won't be surprised. Guys don't do this on their own. Three of them run at the same time with five or six other guys cheering them on, encouraging them, imploring them to go beyond themselves.

They do, running to the point of not being able to take another step, learning to think about something else besides the pain, experiencing for themselves the distinction between act and feel. "We don't take the easy way out and stop the treadmill when we're tired," says midfielder Sheldon Myer.

"We keep going. When other guys were around us, we'd run until we literally fell off the treadmill. Then after that, we'd get right back on."

2011 captain Sam Woodworth comments on the effect: "There were guys who didn't think they had a chance to make it but who did make it because of the encouragement. If they had done it by themselves, they would have hopped off: 'I'm tired, I'm done.' But the last thing you want to do is let your teammates down."

To us it's important to get the last goal in every game of the season. Doing it when it doesn't matter carries over to the times when it does.

Nick Thompson
Class of 2011

Here's the other striking thing about the treadmill parties: For both the men and the women, the runs are optional. NCAA rules prohibit making this sort of thing a requirement in the off-season. But notwithstanding, everybody does them. It goes back to the relationships and the chemistry, what we covered in Discipline 4. Center forward Josh Wood claims that "nobody—*nobody*—misses a run. You are threatening your relationship with the team if you do. If someone has a questionable ailment, a teammate will ask:'Are you really hurt? What's going on?' They're checking whether a guy's becoming mentally-weak. There's a self-governing dimension to all this. People confront under-performance."

Notice, too, that this is the off-season. It's not about fitness for the fall season. It's entirely about young men and women learning that many of their perceived limits are in fact self-imposed. When it comes to developing mental toughness, personal experience is indeed the best teacher.

The same is true for training players to "finish strong." How does that become a habit? By players *experiencing* it each day in practice. In drills and in small-sided games, for example, there's not only an emphasis on scoring goals but also on scoring the last goal of the game. It's even stressed in their camps: Teams get three points for a win, one for a tie and one for scoring the final goal of the game.

2010 captain and All-American Nick Thompson explains: "To us it's important to get the last goal in every game of the season. A lot of times it doesn't mean much on the scoreboard, but everyone wants to get that and we'll talk about it afterward. There's a mentality, a habit that gets created."

They don't bleed into the finish. They finish well. It's a way of thinking that makes a difference. Nick concludes, with wisdom beyond his years: "Doing it when it doesn't matter carries over to the times when it does."

Re-Thinking Keep-Away

Back in the 1960s, Gary Becker, an eventual Nobel Prize winner in economics, postulated a theory about the profound usefulness of "specific training" (training that increases a person's productivity primarily in the organization that trained him) over and above the usefulness of "general training" (training that will increase a person's productivity in any organization.) Although Dr. Becker's name did not come up when Messiah soccer designed its training system, the coaches were clearly thinking like Nobel Laureates. They have a clear vision of what things should look like on the field and they use specific training to get there, focusing incessantly on what will work in their particular system.

That may seem like common sense, but it's an uncommon practice. Coaches need to get past the simplistic notion that unlimited touch drills and games like "keep-away" really help win games. "I guess keep-away is okay in practice," says Coach Frey "but that's not the game. Many think it's all about possession, but that's not the game. We're trying to do things for the sake of attacking—move, probe, create seams. There's a purpose to every drill."

Translation: 4v4 keep-away is "general training" and certainly better than nothing. But 4v4 keep-away where you know that this girl is your 7 and that girl is your winger and there are team agreements about how we'll get from here to the goal—that's "specific training." And it shows up in games.

Like this, for example: "Most of the time when I receive a ball," says Leah Sipe, "I do not have to look up to know where my outside backs will be or where the wingers will be standing." It's difficult to overstate the advantage of that. And it seems that it may become more of an advantage as the program matures. The women's team has lost merely two of their last 101 games, a 96-2-3 record, with both losses coming in the national final. Perhaps that's why Frey can respond so good-naturedly to those who lament the Messiah style of play as predictable and even pedantic. He retorts: "Sure, within a couple games you know what we're going to do, but try to stop us." Lately, only about two percent of their D3 competition can.

Coaches may also need to get past the misconception that "the game is the best teacher." It may not be. Again, to quote Frey: "There's some truth to that, but really? It's a little like throwing a kid a keyboard and thinking that will make him a great writer. He'll figure it out. Not really. I think the game is a really good teacher, but *there's got to be direction*."

That "direction" is a major secret of Messiah's success. It's the sort of direction that's been around since Henry Ford made his first million—direction that seemingly applies to Messiah teams as well as it did to Model T's. And it may benefit other improvement-minded leaders as well. The lesson is this: Standardize the system. Bring order out of chaos. Insist on structure rather than sovereignty. Control what you previously thought was uncontrollable. In Brandt's words, "dictate the options" and then, in Becker's words, "use specific training" to instill those options. Enable people to succeed by linking all training to the match.

It's not the only way to win games, of course—just ask the samba sisters in Sao Paulo—but it sure works well for the guys and girls in Grantham.

Appendix to Discipline 5

Positional Responsibilities and Team Agreements

(excerpted from the men's recruitment packet)

Movement and Qualities for Each Position in the 4-3-3 System

Target: Center forward; highest player in the formation

- Movement: Posts up, checks back to midfield, shows in seam, runs out of middle to flag
- Qualities: Can receive with back to goal, strong, good speed, composed in front of goal

7 (attacking center midfielder): Plays underneath target

- Movement: Checks back to ball in midfield, Ajax run to corner flag, run past target when ball is at target's feet
- Qualities: Hardest working player on the team, skillful, good range, ability to turn, good speed

Wing: Wide player; plays along sideline between target and 7

- Movement: Railroad tracks: up and down, stay wide, hips open, always give then go
- Qualities: Good 1v1 ability, clean first touch, ability to cross, dynamic 1-2

6, 8 (holding center midfielders): Plays behind 7 and in front of center backs

- Movement: Support wing backs, support wings, stay away to switch fields, can play out of position

- Qualities: Ball winner, ability to turn, strong in the air, good vision, ability to shoot from range

Outside Backs: Wide defenders; plays next to center back and behind winger

- Movement: Balance defensively, "hero," step hard defensively, support wings
- Qualities: Wins tackles, good speed, good vision for second targets, quarterback

Center Backs: Central defenders; plays between other center back and outside defender

- Movement: Step hard defensively, balance as second defender
- Qualities: Strong, good in the air, good speed, wins tackles, steps well, solid distribution

Team Agreements
Attacking Principles Based on Position

Players	Messiah Soccer	Typical
Central	Penetrate on the ground through seams	Play long balls in the air
	Turn as much as possible	Play the way you face
	Turn away from a 1-2	Play the second half of a 1-2
	First touch across the body	Receive it with either foot
	Never play a square ball	Play square
Wide	Stay as wide as possible	Stand 10-15 yards in from the sideline
	Staple is a give-go	Staple is give-stand
	Turn back instead of crossing a ball over the end line or to the keeper	Often crosses the ball over the end line or to the keeper (Coach says "unlucky")
Attacking	Disciplined shooting	Undisciplined shooting
	Good shot-on-goal percentage	Low shot-on-goal percentage
	Shots down are the only thing that matters	Getting the shot off is the only thing that matters
	If off balance and can't hit a hard shot low, then make another choice	Shoots off balance and off-target (Coach says "unlucky")
	Possession: forwards are committed to overall team possession	Possession: forwards attack at the expense of losing the ball often
Defensive	One touch transition	Clear the ball or dribble

Team Agreements
Defensive Responsibilities

Target: Pressure center backs

Wingers: Pressure outside backs

7: Pressure holding midfielders

6, 8: Pressure center midfielders

Outside Backs: Step in front of outside midfielders, don't let the forward turn, pressure outside midfielders

Center Backs: Step in front of forwards, don't let the forward turn, pressure forwards

Back Four:

First Defender: Pressure—don't need to win the ball, but you do need to step and make defender predictable

Second Defender: First job is support. Be there in case first defender is beaten. Second job is to step—anticipate and step hard

Third Defender: Balance—typically the outside back who is ready to be the "hero" or sweeper

Discipline 6

Choreograph Game Day

Readiness by Design

What does visiting an art museum have to do with winning a national championship game?

In November 2002, the Messiah men were slated to face Otterbein in the finals in tropical St. Lawrence, New York. Because snow delayed the semi-final games the day before, the NCAA shifted the championship game time from 12:00 to 4:00, giving the teams some additional rest. But Coach Brandt wanted to use that extra time for something more—a team experience. Brad McCarty, then the Assistant Coach, was right on it, pinpointing a local cultural hot spot called the Frederic Remington Art Museum. Says Brad with a shrug: "It was the only thing in town."

Please understand, this is not the The Louvre or The Met we're talking about here. It's a little building (it actually looks more like a house) in a little town paying tribute to a little known regional artist who specialized in depictions of the Nineteenth Century American West. Think cowboys, buffalo, and Pocahontas—or at least her progeny. Now think about 25 college guys touring a place like that on a bitterly-cold upstate New York morning ... in preparation for their 4:00 championship.

It seems baffling and bizarre. It makes no sense. But on second thought, it makes perfect sense to those who understand the Messiah game day philosophy. Stay sharp, stay focused, stay unified. It doesn't much matter what they're doing, as long as they're doing it together.

McCarty remembers it well: "We were trying to create a shared experience and a collective mentality to keep us all thinking the same thing." It may have worked. Later that day, Messiah was on the front foot for most of the match, dominating the final more than the 1-0 score line would suggest. It capped a remarkable year, one where the Falcons only trailed for six minutes during the regular season and six minutes in the post-season.

Readiness on the Road

This wasn't the first unusual team activity while on the road, nor would it be the last. Years earlier, Coach Layton Shoemaker had turned road trips into educational, team-building experiences, visiting places like the Billy Graham Center in Illinois or the Air Force Academy in Colorado. And years after their 2002 folkloric odyssey to Remington, on the eve of the 2006 Final Four in Orlando, another unusual road moment: After the customary, pre-tournament banquet, all the Final Four teams were invited to enjoy a free roller coaster ride at Disney World. And every team partook, except for one. The Messiah men went home to bed. Brandt's perspective? "If you want to go to Disney then I suggest you schedule a trip with the family this summer."

2010 captain Nick Thompson commented on the perplexing genius of his coach: "Dave would just do things and people would ask, 'what are we doing this for?' But then later on they'd get it."

Indeed, in retrospect, there seems to be a consistency and a wisdom in these decisions. "I'm anti-distraction," explains Brandt, a bit pedagogically. "I try to eliminate these and set the team mindset. It's a team agreement (that everyone will buy in)." Sometimes that means saying yes to an obscure museum, sometimes it means saying no to a roller coaster ride. But it always means keeping a collective focus.

We love to be on the road.

Several current players and coaches

There are other elements to their road repertoire as well. Often the guys will set up games in their various hotel rooms and then rotate around to play them. Almost always, the team will also watch a movie in the evening—from the expected (an inspirational sports movie like *Remember the Titans*) to the only-at-Messiah types (for example, *Simon Birch*, the story of a boy whose physical ailments have left him much smaller than all the other kids in town, but who nonetheless has a tremendous influence on his community).

It's just different from many of the other teams they've encountered. While tomorrow's opponents have guys walking down the street to McDonald's at 10 p.m., Messiah is together in a team meeting or in a team devotional or in a competitive card tournament. While other teams are straggling in to breakfast in pairs and threes, Messiah goes for a team walk to loosen their legs and then shows up to breakfast together. While other coaches toss their guys a per diem stipend in the morning and say "enjoy the day, see you at 4:30," Messiah has "team time" planned for all but about an hour of game day.

The pervasive theme in all this, as usual, is "team over individual," a philosophy we've seen throughout this book and that we unpacked specifically in Discipline 4. Says Brandt, the mastermind of the game day milieu: "The team walk stamps 'team over individual.'" But there is balance, he continues. "Some of the time on this trip is for you, some is for us. You don't want it to be a police state, that's not the point. In the end, things like the walk are good things. You'll have time to study, time to hang out and time to do stuff with the team ... Guys understand why the team element is important."

Most of them, anyway. Some will tell you they'd rather sleep in or watch TV or do homework than go for a walk or play a mandatory game of paper football in the next room. But "the overall feeling," according to 2010 grad Trey Overholt, "is that we're having fun together, we're in this together, we're going to battle together."

If that's true, it may partly explain a puzzling statistic. From 2000 to 2010, the men's team lost only 11 home games in those 11 years, but their road record during that time was actually better than their home record—a winning percentage of .924 versus .911. Pretty remarkable, since so many of those road games involved the heightened challenge of the NCAA playoffs.

They could probably dominate in paper football, too.

Readiness at Home

In away games, the women's teams have been equally nettlesome to their opponents, having dropped a paltry six road games from 2000 to 2010. As with the men, they've enjoyed some significant unbeaten streaks away from Shoemaker Field, sometimes stretching for seasons. Also like the men's team, says 2011 captain Kelsey Gorman, "there's very little free time and it's highly scheduled"—focused and often fun. Players and coaches on both teams used this phrase: "We love to be on the road."

But they're also quick to add that there's no better place to play than at "The Shoe." And, true to form, the teams have a standardized routine they follow in preparation for these home games—a routine that also may yield some advantage.

After dressing for the game, the women's team meets about 90 minutes before kickoff for "focus time"—a half-hour of sitting together near the locker room, always in the same spot, always in the same order. Some listen to music, some journal, some pray or read the Bible, but no one talks. It's silent mental preparation. For each athlete, the game has already begun.

They next walk about a quarter mile to "the hut," a structure near the playing field. Striding in pairs, again always next to the same partner, they're silent except for when they break out into a worship song or announce their arrival to the crowd with a prolonged, cacophonous scream as they pass through Messiah's signature covered bridge. In the hut, each slaps the top of the door frame and a small sign. They lace up their boots, sing for ten more minutes, always ending with the same medley song, "I love you, Lord." That's Scott Frey's cue to enter for his brief pre-game talk.

As with so many other elements of this program, they do the same things the same way every time. "It's not superstition," asserts Gorman. "It's just comfortable and it's our tradition."

It may be much more, though. "Those traditions," claims 2005 All-American Hannah (Levesque) Leatherman, "are absolutely vital to the success of the team because they unify the team. They make you feel like you're part of something really big."

That "something" is, in fact, their connection to the past teams on whose shoulders they stand. These women are not just playing for themselves or their coach or their parents or their College or even for their beloved teammates. They're also playing for their predecessors, for every young woman who has made that same walk, yelled through the same bridge, slapped the same door frame and sat in that exact spot singing worship songs. Says Hannah: "It makes a huge difference, more than a person might think."

And, of course, they are playing for the One who gives them the ability to play. This is not just a game; it's nothing less than a spiritual experience for so many of the women whose uniform boldly confesses the Source of their strength. They're playing, as we learned back in Discipline 1, "for something more."

Several elements of The Messiah Method all converge at this moment. The higher purpose. An intentional routine. Athletes who are *both* playing *and* worshipping. An energizing team chemistry. For the men it's much the same at home games, though they have their own distinct traditions.

I'm anti-distraction.
I try to eliminate these and
set the team mindset.

Dave Brandt
Men's Coach, 1997-2008

Three and a half hours before kickoff they eat—basically whatever they want, but the one stipulation is that they eat as a team. They're in the locker room 90 minutes later, getting dressed and beginning their own mental preparation, polishing cleats, occasionally slapping a hand, listening to iPods, clearing their minds. It's subdued, there's no joking around, but it's not quite as delimited as the women's "focus time." The coach comes in 45 minutes before the game and usually offers an animated but brief pep talk. Two by two, then, like the women, they walk to the field—except the men are completely silent the whole way. No singing, no shouting. Just concentration. They huddle at the field, pray, and begin their surprisingly-abbreviated pregame drills. Almost never at home are they the first team on the field.

Their longstanding warm-up music blasts over the loudspeaker, beginning with bagpipes playing *Amazing Grace*. The song resonates throughout the whole campus. Students quicken their pace toward the field. It's just about game time.

The women's and men's routines are just that—habitual, standardized processes. They've been the same for years. Maybe that somehow makes a difference in the game, maybe not. The women I interviewed were more confident about that than were the men.

As every soccer coach knows, though, this is a psychological game as much as it's a physical one. So, as with many other things these teams do, Messiah coaches intentionally manage the team's mentality. They're also very intentional about their own game day preparation. Like their players, the leaders' readiness, as we'll see next, is by design.

Game Day Leadership: Five Habits

Choreography extends to the Messiah coaches. Over the years, they've developed some formidable game day leadership habits that enable them to be at their best before and during the match. Here are five of them.

Invest in the Pregame Talk

There are a number of philosophies about what a team talk should include. For example, in his 2000 autobiography, legendary Manchester United coach, Sir Alex Ferguson, put it this way: "A team talk should always contain a healthy dose of realism, should encourage your men to recognize their strengths and work to exploit them. We have good players and I should give them mature advice about patience, maintaining possession, how to initiate counter-attacks and how to avoid being provoked and led into unproductive activity by the cunning of the opposition."[20]

That's useful, though, I think, not intended to be exhaustive. Every coach has his or her preferred themes. At Messiah, they tend to be topics like staying focused, avoiding complacency, and continually playing to a standard of excellence.

And they tend to be articulated quite professionally. That's, in part, because pregame talks at Messiah are *not improvised*. Our chapter on "Intentionality" (Discipline 2) unpacked this process in some detail. Although these talks are usually only five to ten minutes in length, they're carefully designed and, according to Coach Frey, "semi-rehearsed" so the coach can deliver them cogently. It's a moment that matters, so they invest the time to build it right.

Don't Rely on Emotion

Emotion is overrated as a motivator.

"Some teams play on emotion, but we don't go down that road," says Coach McCarty. "Instead, we talk a lot about steely determination and focus, because that's going to last much longer than emotion. Emotion comes and goes so it's not going to help you day in and day out."

Prudent words. Many veteran coaches get this. But it might be a revelation to others who spend an inordinate amount of time pondering how to get their team "pumped up" for the match.

That's not to say the Messiah coaches don't seek to inspire; they certainly do, as we discuss elsewhere in this book. It is to say, though, that these guys don't expend time trying to arouse game day emotions to gain an edge. Emotional highs are just too fleeting, often dissipating with fatigue or the opponent's first goal.

***Some teams play on emotion,
but we talk a lot about steely determination and focus.
That's going to last much longer than emotion.***

**Brad McCarty
Men's Coach**

Relatedly, Messiah coaches insist that their team not wear their emotions on their sleeve during the match, especially when the other team has momentum. Says Brandt: "We don't want the other team to know whether we're tired or frustrated or scared or surrendering or overconfident or anything else. We don't want the other team to be able to read us and thereby gain any advantage."

It's the upshot of principles like "separate act from feel" and "choose to be positive" (Discipline 5). Coach Frey teaches the women the same thing: "You can't allow your body language to communicate you're tired or down … Our emotions, our feelings, our concerns about injustice can put us at a competitive disadvantage if the opponent can read us."

Overall, the Messiah philosophy seems to be that emotion is more an enemy than a friend. So they often treat it that way.

Motivate Through Reframing

Here's a better motivation strategy, a shrewd one used pervasively in this program. It's called "reframing."

In the context of communication, it means to help people see old things in new ways by changing their frame of reference. And that can make a big difference since changed thinking almost automatically leads to changed behavior.

A prime example: Frey's practice of soliciting soccer alumnae to write letters to the current team. As the alums reflect on what they miss and what, with the clarity of hindsight, *really* matters in the soccer program, it reframes the season for the team—and it sometimes reframes the game day moment, when the letter is used that way. They're reminded of how precious and ephemeral their college career is. They're reminded to enjoy themselves and their relationships. They're reminded that the higher purposes should eclipse the momentary concerns of scores and rankings and personal reputation.

Here's another potent example of reframing, though significantly less subtle. In 2001, Stockton College won the D3 Men's National Championship—on Messiah's field nonetheless. From the bleachers, an exasperated Falcons squad, who had just fallen in the semis to Redlands, watched Stockton sit on their bench, storm their field and cut down their nets.

The next season, Messiah would go head to head with the defending champs at Stockton's field. Brandt essentially wanted one thing from his boys—for them to attack relentlessly. But he didn't just tell them. He and his assistants plastered the locker room wall with 200 sheets of paper that said "ATTACK" in the largest possible font. When the boys walked in, the point was obvious.

Brandt was attempting to reframe what could have been a daunting situation. No longer was it Messiah taking on the defending national champs. It was a 90 minute all-out assault on their goal. And after those 90 minutes, a stunning score line: a four-nil pasting of the home team.

Here's some more reframing. Later that year, because Messiah had been upset in their conference finals, they needed a play-in game against a talented and tough Johns Hopkins side to make the NCAA tournament. Besides that, to survive the first-round weekend, they'd also need to beat two top-12 teams, Salisbury and perennial powerhouse Greensboro.

"We were unbelievable," recalls Brandt. "We trailed for only six minutes all year long, but we got this horrendous draw (into what everyone was calling) the group of death."

His approach to the seeming injustice? Reframe the situation. "The only way we can play this," he concluded, "is as the underdog. So I grabbed the underdog mantle and ran with it."

That sort of reframing may have been quite effective. Defender Kevin Schneider said this about the underdog perspective: "It ... relieved us of the pressure to win ... It was great going into games with confidence and maybe some anger that the other team was expected to win."[21]

Messiah survived the weekend, winning those three games in four days, and was rewarded by hosting the next round, one that included a match with Drew University, the third-ranked D3 team in the country. Because Drew was the higher-seeded team, their coach called Brandt with a rogue request: Drew wanted to wear white and sit on Messiah's home bench.

"I went to my team with that and they were incredulous, but it played right into my hands. I embraced it." It fit perfectly the template of disrespected underdog. Next, Brandt brilliantly treated this as a road game, getting lodging for his team in a nearby Hershey hotel, having the team visit Hershey's Chocolate World the night before, and taking them through the rest of their typical away-game routine.

The next day, the blue-shirted underdog knocked off the white-shirted favorites in overtime, another step toward what would eventually become their second national title.

Reframing—helping people see anew—is a powerful leadership tool. It can happen through stories and through metaphors. Or sometimes it simply involves a fresh thought that changes perspective and eases the tension. Coach Layton Shoemaker would occasionally say in tense moments: "Don't worry; God already knows who's going to win." Other times a mere word, like "underdog" or "attack," if it's shared pervasively, can alter team thinking and influence results.

Any leader can use this motivational tool, and in fact most do, at least occasionally. But here's a tip from some pretty successful coaches: You might want to grab it from the toolbox more often.

Divide Halftime into Two Halves

The midway point of a match is where a soccer coach really earns his or her money. "Do we need to change the formation?" says Coach Frey. "Are we getting exposed defensively anywhere? Is there a match-up we're not taking advantage of? Are there choices that we aren't making that we should?"

Formation? Personnel? Strategy? Work rate? Motivation? "What are the couple things they need to hear out of the thousand we could talk about?" asks Assistant Men's Coach Aaron Faro, summarizing the challenge.

The coaches don't just dive in with advice at the half. They're more judicious about this weighty moment, wanting to get it right. So, as Faro explains, "For the first fifty to seventy percent of halftime, the coaches meet with each other while the guys do the same on their own." In the leadership huddle, the Assistants, who have been tasked with scouting the other side for the opening 45, share their insights. The Head Coach, who has primarily kept mental notes, floats his ideas. They quickly identify the best mid-course corrections.

Meanwhile, a few feet away, these seven or eight minutes of "team time" is not wasted time. It's genuine self-diagnosis and remediation according to 2010 captain Katie Hoffsmith, a veteran of more than 100 halftimes in four years. "We talk about switching fields more, finding 6 more, or anything else that needs to change. If I'm not connecting with the wing, I'll specifically go over and talk to her." But then, 2011 captain Kelsey Gorman adds: "Once we see Coach walking over, everyone gets silent no matter what we're talking about. There's a lot of respect. It's not demanded; it just happens."

This is seldom an emotional time, consistent with the stoic tenor of pregame. It's not a jovial time or a panicky time, no matter the score. Just business."Steely determination."

And as much as they make specific adjustments, the coaches' words to the team are often general and inspirational. "We don't talk about the score much," says Faro. "Sometimes we need to call out guys or speak specifically to them. But often, halftime is just putting the standard in front of them again: Commit to excellence. It's really evident at halftime."

Again the reframing. This is not about the scoreboard and not primarily about winning. It's foremost about excellence. "Playing to a standard," as they like to say. Focus on playing your game the way you've been trained to play it.

Admittedly, what the Messiah coaches do at the half may seem a bit unremarkable. But what might be instructive is that it too is designed—there's a choreography to it all. They split the half in half. In doing so, the coaches give themselves the time to make better decisions, they afford players the time to teach and influence one another, and overall, they leverage the collective brainpower of the group.

Prioritize On-the-Job Training

"When I first started as head coach," recalls Scott Frey, "we used to play 13 players deep—maybe. Now it's more like 18 deep in a game."

It's a useful strategy for many reasons. For one thing, injuries become less debilitating since players with some experience can step in. For another, if they don't "play deep," says Frey, "it creates an 'us-and-them' mindset in practice. But if we have 18 to 20 playing per game, then everyone thinks that practice matters and they work hard. Plus relationships improve because everyone knows they're important and they matter and they'll play."

A more obvious advantage of playing many of the reserves is that it can yield a competitive edge during the match. The men's team has employed this approach for years, with up to 20 players seeing action for at least 30 minutes per game. And more recently under Coach McCarty, sometimes five or six subs will enter simultaneously, like a line change in hockey, leaving sportswriters, broadcasters, and the other bench scrambling to check the roster. It causes opposing players to scramble as well, suddenly confronted by a dozen fresh legs—a competitive edge indeed.

But the frequent substitution strategy is about more than enhancing commitment or exhausting their opponents. It's also about far-sighted preparation.

Messiah is not only playing to win today, they're using today's game to help them win the next one. And to win the games next month. And in the post-season. And the games next year, for that matter. Today's game is more than a must-win to stay atop the rankings. It's on-the-job training for the reserves.

I don't ever want to be young.
I just want it to be another new group. But that's an intentional decision by the coaches.

Scott Frey
Women's Coach

Of course, bench strength makes this possible, a derivative of their "both-and" recruiting (Discipline 3), the "team chemistry" that lures away top prospects from D1 programs (Discipline 4), and their intense, specific training for every player (Discipline 5). The men's squad has even become so deep that in overtime, they'll sometimes start six players from their second team to give their first team an extra five minutes' rest before they explode off the bench.

Like everything else in their game day leadership, this is all by design. It happens because of a premeditated decision. "I don't ever want to be young," says Frey about his team. "I just want it to be another new group. But that's an intentional decision by the coaches."

It's also an echo of his old coach, Layton Shoemaker, who imparts with a knowing confidence that "good programs don't have rebuilding years." No, they prepare next year's players on the pitch this year.

An Environment that Enables Execution

Away game camaraderie. Home game routines. Effective game day leadership. It doesn't just happen. Most of this is closely managed. As usual, intentionality and attention to detail are touchstones of success.

Of all the elements in the Messiah Method, though, this one may have the most indeterminate nexus between processes and results. To an objective observer, it's simply difficult to know whether or how much these practices influence the final score.

The leaders seem pretty certain, so they continue to invest heavily in these routines. They're striving to create an environment where execution is more likely. No small matter. Men's keeper coach Aaron Schwartz sums it up well: "You can teach somebody all sorts of things. If they can't apply it, it's just not gonna happen."

That may sound self-evident, but leaders in every walk of life ignore these simple truths. To win you have to execute. Execution requires readiness. And readiness is no accident. At Messiah, it happens through purposeful, road-tested processes—both home and away, both before and during the match—that culminate in peak performance.

At Messiah, they choreograph game day so they can execute with excellence.

Discipline 7

Play to a Standard

The Secret to Sustaining Success

"It's a tough standard you create when you finish number two in the country and you're disappointed. That's a tough world to live in."

Scott Frey was both philosophical and poignant at the press conference following the 2010 championship game. His team had just completed another head-turning season, coming into the championship having scored 114 goals while yielding only three.

But unthinkably, they gave up two in the first five minutes of the final, both on corners, and then had to chase the game from there. Despite a cracking second half goal by freshman Alicia Frey (yes, the coach's daughter) on a precision pass from sophomore All-American Alex Brandt (yes, the other coach's daughter), Messiah could not find an equalizer. Like 2002 and 2007, it would be a runner-up year for the Messiah women.

There are more than 400 women's soccer programs in Division III. So why be disappointed with second in the nation?

One might think that it's because Messiah is so accustomed to winning. Prior to this game, these women had gone undefeated for 76 straight and were beaten only once in their last 100 games. In fact, most of the team—the freshmen, sophomores and juniors—had *never* lost a game in a Messiah uniform.

That's not really it, though. There's more to the disappointment than simply the novelty of losing. And once we understand why they set the bar so high, we'll also understand their secret for sustaining success, a habit that can take any team and any organization to the next level—and keep them there.

Recall from our chapter on Purpose (Discipline 1) that for this women's team, as well as for the Messiah men's team, winning is not the primary objective. They have higher purposes, one of which is to play with excellence all the time. As Coach Brandt said in 2006 after three straight titles: "We hope to win, but we focus on striving for excellence, which is more under our control than winning."[22]

That's an important distinction. Throughout the years, these teams have not focused on victories or trophies. Foremost, they're focused on continuous improvement, on getting better and better each game, on achieving their potential not just one year or some years or usually, but *all the time*—every season, every game, even every touch of the ball.

Brandt's description encapsulates it: They are "striving for excellence." And Scott Frey is right there with him: "We strive for perfection even though it's not going to happen in soccer. The closer we get, the better we are."

It transcends seasons, too. When they finish second, the striving continues. And when they finish first, the striving continues.

Think about how important that is. How do these teams make it to the Final Four every year (or, to be precise, every year except once from 2000 to 2010 for both the men's team and the women's team)? How can the men's team boast a playoff record during this time period that's actually *better* than their regular season record? And how can the women go unbeaten for seasons at a time?

It's largely because of the culture of continuous improvement, the relentless pursuit of higher quality play. It's a mindset that there is no finish line, that they've never arrived, that even after winning it all, they can still become even better.

In Messiah language, they sustain success year after year by "playing to a standard."

Play to a Standard

Many leaders and many teams claim to prioritize "excellence." But few achieve the kind of ongoing success this soccer program has. To quote Cory Furman, Messiah's current Assistant Athletics Director for Media Relations, "*how in the name of Dave Brandt does this keep happening?*"

When asked that way, the question practically answers itself. Brandt is indeed the architect of Messiah's strategy for sustained excellence. Influenced heavily in this regard by his father, former Messiah College Dean Dave Brandt, Sr., and by the man he calls a "second father figure," 23-year Head Coach Layton Shoemaker, excellence has long been a way of life for Coach Brandt.

However, in early 2004, as he tells it, he became acutely aware of a potential threat to long-term success. Ironically, it was the success itself—what Brandt claims "could be the very undoing of the team. Nothing breeds complacency faster than a few national titles."

The same is true in any organization. Being good—and even more so, being the best—can create a stumbling block to remaining there. Number Two is typically hungrier than Number One and works harder to attain the top spot.

Playing to a standard is probably the biggest secret to our repeated success.

Dave Brandt
Men's Coach, 1997-2008

That's exactly where the men's team was after the 2003 season, having won the D3 titles in 2000 and 2002, but having not yet repeated. Says Brandt: "Reaching the goal creates an inevitable drop in motivation, drop in vision, and drop in focus, and that can become the year we lose … I wanted to avoid that inconsistency."

He knew that a reframing was in order.

So Brandt adopted a breakthrough idea: We will "play to a standard" all the time and that standard will be perfection—the game where every pass connects, every run is well-timed, every shot rips the back of the net. He explains in retrospect: "We aimed to play the perfect game, always striving for more, always playing to that standard. The team ultimately believed that when we had the ball, if we chose correctly and we executed, you couldn't stop us."

That's not meant to be arrogant, just aspirational. The ideal, in games and in practices, is to play flawlessly. And over the years it's become a mantra, a term that's probably used more than any other within the Messiah soccer program. In training, before games, at halftime, in private conversations, and in a player's own self-talk, the mantra resounds: "play to a standard." Whether they're down a goal or up by five, they play to the same standard. Whether it's a pre-season scrimmage or the Final Four, play to a standard.

It's even manifest in the annual spring match against the alumni, where the teams are beating the tar out of one another, scrapping for every loose ball, tackling their hardest, working at full intensity for all 90 minutes. "Every team is supposed to leave the program better than they found it," says current midfield standout Sheldon Myer. "So the best way we can honor the alums is by kicking the crap out of them."

Clearly, as one of Sheldon's mentors, Assistant Coach Troy Sauer, says in summary: "At Messiah there's no such thing as a simple pick-up game." Not when you're persistently playing to a standard.

The Melody in His Head

It's impossible to overstate the value of that collective mindset. In fact, it's sought by world-class organizations around the globe. The bar is up here, we're down here, let's do whatever it takes to close the gap. When every team member buys-in to that kind of thinking, it eviscerates complacency and supercharges results.

Whom does Brandt credit for the innovation? Not Alex Ferguson or Anson Dorrance or Louis Van Gaal or Vince Lombardi or even Jim Collins—men who have influenced him so profoundly over the years. Instead, he cites Bono, the front man for the rock band U2, another team that has sustained success for decades in the face of accelerating competition.

By the late 1980's, U2 had achieved a significant amount of commercial success. In fact, they had become quite rich and famous and began asking one another, "Can we relax now?" Bono, the band's leader, reportedly answered that question with wisdom: "We can relax, but if we do, we'll become irrelevant." He later added: "If you judge success by the fact that we can afford to buy this house, it's a dangerous measure. I judge success by how close we are to the melody I hear in my head."

The melody in his head. That became a moving metaphor for Brandt, a reconceptualization of "success" to be something other than getting to the top. It meant getting there and *staying* there, or at least playing to the team's potential all the time. It meant an ultimate vision that "is a higher calling than winning."

"Most people—and you do this without thinking about it," claims Brandt, "naturally play to one thing and that's winning." He wanted his teams instead to "play to a standard," the better melody for long-term success.

It makes complete sense and it's entirely transferrable to almost any leadership situation, if the leader is willing to adopt a new paradigm. It's essentially a vision of the unattainable ideal and then an incessant quest to get as close as possible.

And what in the name of Dave Brandt were the results? They could hardly be better. From the 2004 season, when Brandt more deliberately began communicating this idea, through the 2010 season, the Messiah men went to every Final Four and won every national title except one. Little wonder that Brandt calls playing to a standard "probably the biggest secret to our repeated success."

At Messiah there's no such thing as a simple pick-up game.

Troy Sauer
Class of 2003, Men's Assistant Coach

Moreover, it's not been just a guy thing. Scott Frey has adopted the same concept, also with remarkable success. "Our girls know that we'll never arrive. We'll never play the perfect game. But we're going to try to. Even though we know we can't achieve it, that doesn't mean we don't pursue it."

The women's program even uses the same language here. Frey continues: "We play to a standard. When we play and train, it is so irrelevant what anybody else in the world is doing. I don't care what this team or that program has done. It's all about us and what we can achieve."

Also, like Brandt, Frey too has a melody in his head. "What's the standard? It's me. It's what I think they're capable of doing. I have the vision for what I want it to look like ... and we'll never get there, but we're going to try like crazy to get as close as we can."

In light of these results, Brandt's advice to leaders is as prudent as it is predictable: Think huge. Think idealistically. Much bigger than what might be achievable today or tomorrow. He counsels, with his trademark directness: "If there's no melody in your head, then it's possible your leadership lacks vision. If there once was a melody but you've forgotten about it, I encourage you to reinvest in that idealism."

"The Dogged Pursuit of Excellence"

That melody at Messiah has long included "excellence" in its chorus. And from the program's early days through today, it's been a repetitious song.

In this regard, both Brandt and Frey make their liberal arts alma mater proud by quoting Aristotle: "We are what we repeatedly do. Excellence, then, is not an act but a habit." The 2,400 year old wisdom translates well in central Pennsylvania. Giving one's best at all times is a lifestyle, a tradition, even an addiction in these programs. They call it "the dogged pursuit of excellence" and it touches everything from their work ethic to fitness to technical skills to soccer IQ to character to relationships to academics. "Playing to a standard"—and in their case, living to a standard—means doing everything with utmost quality and distinction.

And it's had staying power in the Messiah soccer program, maybe more so than it might have in other places, because it comports with their worldview. You see, pursuing excellence does not just derive from a U2 quote or from benchmarking the best teams or from reading books on Six-Sigma quality. It also comes from another bestselling Book. At Messiah, "the dogged pursuit of excellence" is both their theory of long-term success and their theology.

It's a straightforward teaching, beginning with their shared belief that they're to do everything for God. That's Discipline 1 in this book because it's discipline one in the lives of these men and women. Messiah players and coaches seek to be "good stewards" of the gifts God has accorded them. Essentially, their mindset is: "If God has called me to do this, who am I to do it with anything less than excellence?"

This is a longstanding philosophy in the program, dating back to Layton Shoemaker, the men's coach from 1974-1996. Many interviewees had referred to it, so over breakfast, I asked Shoemaker about the theology. "If you're going to label something 'Christian,'" he told me with an intensity unbecoming of the diner toast and coffee between us, "then you've got to do it with excellence."

He then punctuated his statement: "Or don't do it at all."

If you're going to label something "Christian," then you've got to do it with excellence. Or don't do it at all.

Layton Shoemaker
Men's Coach, 1974-1996

No doubt, this is among the man's passions, having laid the groundwork for a continuous improvement culture that's bridged generations and genders. 1984 grad Dan Haines enthuses that "Layton really instilled in us the quest for excellence—whatever you do, you must do it right." 2008 grad Jennifer Myhre phrases it this way: "Soccer is a way to worship, as God gave us the talents to be used for His glory." And 2011 grad Mark Jeschke told the media: "To play for the glory of God (means) … to play to a standard of excellence, and it affects virtually everything we do."[23]

It appears that for sacred as well as strategic reasons, good is not good enough. And, truth be told, neither is a national championship. Trophy in hand, there's still more excellence to pursue, more stewardship to perform, more melody to sing.

Lofty aspirations. But they've also become lasting realities. We'll turn next to how they do it.

From Decent to Dynasty: Some Practical Advice for Continuous Improvement

Though they never reached the NCAA post-season before Frey took the helm, the women's program went 27-8-1 in its two seasons preceding his appointment, and had an overall winning percentage of .608 since its inception in 1988. The men's program had also been successful for years before promoting Brandt to the top spot, earning a .751 winning percentage under Coach Shoemaker, and making the NCAA's half the years since it joined in 1981, including two Final Four appearances. They'd also won the National Christian College Athletic Association title twice, in 1978 and 1981.

But led by Brandt and Frey, and later by McCarty, they broke through, leveraging the whole system of disciplines described in this book. And importantly, they stayed at the top, going from decent to dynasty, ultimately becoming the winningest college soccer program in America from 2000 to 2010.

By contrast, the Final Four teams they've faced along the way made it there only occasionally, usually once. "It's a little like catching a butterfly," says Dave Brandt, expressing what might be his favorite metaphor. They fly a bit erratically and if you grab at it, you might catch it every fifth or sixth time. "That's the way many soccer programs are," according to Brandt. "Every once in a while, they have *that year* when everything goes right."

Messiah, though, has found a way to catch the butterfly—to reach its enormous potential—almost every season in recent memory. Concepts like "playing to a standard" and "the dogged pursuit of excellence" have been instrumental in this regard, staving off the complacency and smugness that breeds former champions.

The question remains, though: *What does this look like in practical terms?* It's one thing to create inspirational language about a better future; it's quite another to deliver on it.

Earlier in this book, we encountered some answers to this question. For example, they elevate their game through "standard-bearers" who lead their peers to new levels (Discipline 4), through off-season "treadmill parties" (Discipline 5), and through the habit of "finishing strong" by always seeking the last goal (Discipline 5).

But that's a mere sampling. Messiah has several other road-tested methods for continuous improvement. Here are five powerful ones that any leader can adopt.

Repetition

Sir Alex Ferguson, long-time head coach of perennial contenders Manchester United, writes this in his autobiography:

> "[G]ood coaching relies on repetition. Forget all the nonsense about training programmes to keep players happy. The argument that they must be stimulated by constant variety may come across as progressive or enlightened, but it is a dangerous evasion of priorities. In any physical activity, effective practice requires repeated execution of the skill involved. Why do you think the greatest golfers who have ever lived have devoted endless hours to striking the same shots over and over again? Yes, I know golf, where the ball always sits to be struck, is so different from football that technical comparisons are foolish. But the link is the need to concentrate on refining technique to the point where difficult skills become a matter of habit.

> "When footballers complain about dullness of repetitive passing exercises, it is usually not monotony they resent, but hard work. David Beckham is Britain's finest striker of a football not because of a God-given talent but because he practices with a relentless application that the vast majority of less gifted players wouldn't contemplate. Practice may not make you perfect, but it will definitely make you better and any player working with me on the training ground will hear me preach the virtues of repetition—repeatedly."[24]

It sounds like an echo of Aristotle: "we are what we repeatedly do." There's a profundity in this idea that transcends time.

It transcends countries, too—from Greece to Great Britain to Grantham, PA. Repetition is at the heart of the Messiah training program. That's actually an understatement. More accurate might be that it's in the middle of the epicenter of the bulls-eye.

My collection of drills
wouldn't be that thick of a book.

Dave Brandt
Men's Coach, 1997-2008

So the daily drills are very familiar. Some of them were yesterday's drills, too. And tomorrow's. Recall Coach Brandt's words that we first encountered in Discipline 5: "my collection of drills or exercises wouldn't be that thick of a book." Consequently, the players often know what the coaches will say before they say it. They also know the coach will run an exercise until the team gets it right. That's the whole point. Repetition begets excellence, but only when a coach has the tenacity to stick with the drill until it genuinely affects skill level, teamwork and flow.

This is no small matter in a world replete with, as Ferguson laments, "training programmes to keep players happy." The focus is entirely on developing technical and tactical abilities that improve their form in a game situation. If a player has a problem with the repetitive nature of the training, "tough luck" says an unapologetic Dave Brandt. "This is the way we do it. This is what makes us excellent." Tenacity personified.

Frankly, this approach might be a little dull for coaches as well, adds Scott Frey. "We're doing things in a repetitive manner that happen on the field often. We instill the basics and then the situation. It's sometimes boring for the coaches, but we often add new ideas."

Amusement is beside the point, though. Again, this is not entertainment. It's training. These coaches know the difference on the practice field.

And they know the difference in their summer camps. Sometimes the camps, too, get a bad rap according to 1980's captain Greg Clippinger who's worked the Messiah camps for decades. "Some say the camps are too structured and boring—that there's too much repetition. Some say they're not enough fun—that kids have to work too hard. But in the end, it makes kids better players."

It also makes them repeat customers, with well over fifteen hundred boys and girls now attending each summer. Messiah continues to see a steady stream of returning campers, despite rising camp prices and fluctuations in the economy.

Interestingly, perhaps, Brandt's bottom line on all this comes from an academic article, a further testimony to his breadth of knowledge. He quotes from a journal called *Sociological Theory*: "Excellence is accomplished through the doing of actions, ordinary in themselves, performed consistently and carefully, habitually compounded together, added up over time."

Ordinary actions, performed consistently, performed carefully. That captures well the Messiah training philosophy. The title of the article may capture it even better: "The Mundanity of Excellence."[25]

Set and Enforce High Expectations

Next to Coach Frey at that difficult, end-of-the-season press conference sat Erin Hench, the 2009 Player of the Year, and Amanda Naeher, the 2008 and 2010 Player of the Year. All of them had sat in those chairs before under happier circumstances. At one point, Hench made a succinct but striking comment to the media: "We get two weeks off now." Naeher nodded with a smile, adding: "We get Christmas break … maybe."

Coach Frey corroborated his stars: "Erin's right. In two or three weeks, we're going to start all over again because that's what it takes. That's the reality. To sit here on this day—they started last January."

These coaches are constantly pushing, more than 11 months out of the year. They set high expectations, they enforce high expectations. And it makes everyone a lot better than they would be otherwise.

We strive for perfection even though it's not going to happen in soccer. The closer we get, the better we are.

Scott Frey
Women's Coach

It may be most evident on the practice field. Nobody is allowed to just go through the motions when training, says Todd Suessmuth, one of Messiah's leading goal scorers. "They don't take anything lightly, even if it's just a drill in practice. That drill can make the difference between scoring a goal or not scoring a goal in a game; between saving a goal and not saving a goal. Their training has gotten them to the point where everything has to be taken 100 percent seriously."

Coach Brandt clarifies that no one is exempt: "There's a lot of calling out of players in hundreds of small situations, but it's dictated by the vision. I know how I want it to look and I think it's a good vision. And I'm not going to fold to our best players because they want to do it their way."

No accommodation for four-time All-Americans or any other standouts? No additional chances? Brandt is unequivocal about this. Frey may allow a bit of a longer leash for critical players, based on some of his experiences at Alma College and at Messiah, but in the end, he too insists on the standard from everyone.

Enforcement matters. But many leaders fear its consequences, so they back off.

Bad idea, says Brandt. Fatal, in fact. "There's an insecurity in leaders. But you have to say 'we're never going to fold to the individual.' You have to be uncompromising in this. It can't matter if some recruit doesn't come or if some guy quits the team."

High standards consistently enforced. It's hardly revolutionary, though it can culminate in revolutionary results. In fact, no college soccer coach at any level has a higher winning percentage than Brandt. So his challenge to leaders is worth heeding: "Take up the battle of moving the people under you out of the comfort zone to which they will always naturally lean to."

Measure Twice, Correct Once

All teams keep stats, some more than others, of course. There's variance within the Messiah program as well, with the women's team taking a somewhat casual approach while the men's team has elevated measurement to a sacrament.

One thing these coaching staffs do have had in common, though, is their reluctance to simply trust their gut about how their players are performing. They may think someone had a poor game, for example, and needs to make certain adjustments, but they'll usually check the video first before having that conversation.

"I'll look at the video to see whether my perception is true," says Frey. "Is she really losing the ball all the time? Is she just trying to do too much? Or is she only losing it when trying to do something really special?" In one instance he was livid about a defender's alleged miscue that led to conceding a goal and, in his words, he "steamed on it for days." But before addressing it with the player, Frey reviewed the video. As it turns out, someone else had made the mistake.

It's a standard practice for Frey. Check first, correct later. "If we give up a goal or something else bad happens, I'll go back and look at the video. As it turns out, my perception of what happened seldom matches what really happened."

That's an unusually humble posture, one that more leaders need to adopt. It's been adopted a few doors down in the men's soccer office as well.

Charting a game is "really helpful from a coaching perspective," says Assistant Men's Coach Aaron Faro. "Sometimes we think a guy has had a good or bad game, but the stats tell a different story. It also helps by reducing misunderstandings between coach and player when corrective action is taken."

Indeed. Everyone's looking at the same thing. It's hard to argue with physical evidence. So there's more buy-in from the player about the necessary adjustments. And better adjustment decisions by coaches in the first place.

That's the typical Messiah way: They measure twice and correct once. It's instrumental for real improvement.

What gets measured? For a fully-charted game, it's minutes played, passes attempted, passes completed, shots, shots on goal, quality crosses, tackles won, blocked shots, head balls won, balls lost to the trap, and balls lost to the dribble. *For each player.* Then there's an overall rating for the positives and the negatives, and an aggregate quantification of each individual's performance.

It's a matter of going through the video, clipboard in hand, and making tally marks. Sounds labor-intensive, but the coaches claim to be able to do it in less than real time, fast-forwarding when the ball goes out of play.

Frey says he "might chart a full game only once a year" for the whole team. Instead, he usually takes a more targeted approach: "I do it on an individual basis (i.e., computing these stats for just one player) because there's something specific I want to see."

In sharp contrast, the men's coaches chart every game for every player. Beyond that, for years they've publicly posted the results after each game in the locker room. The guys are okay with it. "Those analysis sheets are like our report card," says 2010 grad Trey Overholt. "If you have a bad game, people see that, but it's an internal motivator, not a public shame. It's similar to the five minute mile. However, those numbers are also a confidence builder when things are going right."

But the women were decidedly *not* okay with it when, years ago, Frey posted his Excel spreadsheet. They just received it differently, he says, "so I stopped."

Assistant Women's Coach Todd Balsbaugh elaborated: "They're fiercely competitive, but for them to be set apart near the bottom as an individual? That messes with their head. In the male mind, if I'm in last place then I've got to do something about it. In the female mind, if I'm in last place, then that means I'm not good enough. It's a real mental burden for them."

Hence the current practice on the women's side of limiting individual feedback to private conversations. It's an important distinction that leaders may need to respect, one we'll consider further in our next chapter. Many coaching techniques work exceedingly well across the Messiah teams. Some, though, do not. "We're motivated by different things," says Balsbaugh after ten years in the role, "and coaches need to be sensitive to this."

That's not to discount the importance of measurement; it's just some counsel about how coaches should use the data. Overall, the celebrated management adages resonate through these programs: *Measurement matters. You can't manage what you don't measure. Always do a postmortem. Don't trust your gut.*

No, it's better to measure twice—in real time and through video—and correct once.

Play Stretch Competition in the Off-Season

We get better by playing people who are better than we are.

This is a basic axiom of growth, germane to almost any endeavor. And it's one wholeheartedly embraced by the Messiah squads. As Layton Shoemaker, the pioneer of this practice, explained: "Stretching ourselves always makes us better, so we've done a lot of that."

In addition to their three trips to Brazil, the women's team has started to take on Division I schools in the spring, in particular, Bucknell and Penn State. The men's team has long done the same during their spring season, dating back to the 1970s. With their graduating seniors on the sideline, the men have competed against D1 teams like Maryland, Georgetown, Delaware, Lehigh and Penn State—sometimes tying or even winning—as well as playing some sterling competition in Holland, Belgium, Germany, Sweden, Austria and most recently Columbia. As one Facebook post said after the South America trip, "you know you've played a high-level opponent when you play great and lose 5-0 in the tournament championship." Suessmuth, who joined the team on this trip, told me it was the best team they've faced in 30 years.

That's by design. Many of these trips are indeed about ambassadorship and some are specifically missions-oriented (Discipline 1), but they're also about pushing the standard even higher. Whereas some teams might shy away from stretch competition, concerned about demoralizing results and possible injuries, Messiah thrives on it. They learn from it. Like so many of their other habits, this improves their form while keeping them mindful that there's still more room for improvement.

In two or three weeks, we're going to start all over again because that's what it takes. To sit here on this day—they started last January.

Scott Frey an hour after the 2010 National Championship game

Learning and Reinvention

Coach Brandt pointed me to binders standing at attention at his Naval Academy desk, each within reach of his right hand. "There's my Dorrance folder, next to that's Van Gaal, and then Alex Ferguson, there's my U2 folder, Lombardi, and then *Good to Great*. It's all right there. It doesn't go far from me."

Coaches, a rock star and a business guru. Garnished with some assorted academic articles. Quite an eclectic mix of influences. Is it any wonder that one former player extolled him as "a mad scientist with a soccer clipboard"?

Recall also from a previous chapter (Discipline 5) how Brandt marinated himself in the Dutch system, taping Ajax games and then breaking them down, reading everything he could find on the Dutch style of play, visiting Holland with his team, and even going to coaching school there. Great leaders are great learners. And as such, they can reinvent the future.

That's just what Brandt did in 1997, but he continued to do so throughout his time as Messiah's top man. For example, just a few short pages ago we heard about him inventing a clever solution to complacency: "play to a standard." And every week at Messiah he learned from his assistant coaches and from Scott Frey. Says Brandt: "I desperately need a sounding board who's intelligent and knows what's going on. As sure of myself as I am, I'm not sure of myself." Now, he's reinventing again in his new job at Navy, where it seems the 4-3-3 is just not going to work.

Scott Frey has similar attributes, having also gleaned from coaches abroad while benchmarking eminent U.S. programs like Duke, UNC ... and the Messiah men's program. Over the years, Messiah Women's Soccer has leaned rather heavily on its older sibling for best practices—a history symbolized in the cover photo for this book. "We're about two years behind them now," says Frey expectantly, referring to both the men's systems and their playoff dominance.

Like Brandt, Frey reinvented his program by first having the humility to learn.

Coach McCarty has done the same, apprenticing under Brandt for eight years and, in his words, "learning more (in this time) than all of his other soccer experiences combined." He also does a lot of reading in psychology, seeking cutting edge ideas that can keep the team motivated and moving forward.

And decades earlier than any of this (indeed before McCarty was even born), Coach Shoemaker was also making learning a top priority. "One of the best things I did," recalls Shoemaker, "was to go to the first-ever coaching school in this country" led by the famed West German footballer Dettmar Cramer. Shoemaker also pored over John Wooden books during these years, adapting those philosophies to the early Messiah squads. He launched something in 1974 that would within five seasons win the fledgling Messiah program an NCCAA title.

There are two lessons in all this for improvement-minded leaders—lessons that go beyond the ubiquitous advice to "sharpen the saw." First, *adopt a lifestyle of learning* to stay current and to stay a step ahead of the competition. These coaches always have their radar up. They're always on the lookout for fresh, new ideas as well as older, battle-tested techniques. For example, when I mentioned to Brandt in our interview that his standardization approach (Discipline 5) reminded me of W. Edwards Deming, one of the leading management thinkers of the Twentieth Century, Brandt immediately gave me a quizzical look and wrote down on his note pad "Deming—standardization." He had identified a potential new source of knowledge.

The second lesson is to *simplify your learning*. Focus it. Each of these Messiah coaches seems to have been influenced by relatively few thinkers, but relatively deeply. And they continue to access those ideas, repeatedly picking the brains of the same smart people, re-reading the same books year after year. Brandt even recalls reading an Anson Dorrance book four times during a four day soccer convention because "I knew this book would change everything for me."

This is the power of learning, an essential habit for those pursuing the next level. And the habit becomes even more essential once you get there, once you start winning consistently. Everyone has you under their microscope; everyone has your game circled on their calendar. Stand still and you're yesterday's champion. Keep learning and you can invent new ways to win.

Choose Courage over Capitulation

Back at the 2010 post-game press conference, the winning coach that day, Marcus Wood, heaped praise on Scott Frey and the Messiah women: "What's remarkable is they've sustained success. Anyone can do it one time. But that many Final Fours consecutively? And knowing how tough it is to get there one time?"

Getting there once takes talent. Getting there repeatedly? That takes talent and *courage*.

In particular, leadership courage. Why? Because sustaining success entails change—a radical, cultural change from "winning" being the goal to "excellence" or even "perfection" being the goal. Change, in turn, provokes resistance and overcoming resistance requires courage. Bold leadership. A willingness to stand firm in the face of those vested in the status quo.

For years, Frey had been ratcheting up the standard, pushing the girls to their potential, insisting on curfews, escalating fitness demands, requiring a D1 commitment in a D3 program, sometimes to the chagrin of players, parents, and prospects. He's been courageous enough to sustain excellence.

For his part, Coach Brandt, too, has encountered a plethora of push-back—from Messiah alums who want their almost-good-enough kids to make the team, to players who simply don't want to yield, to parents who dislike his methods.

Sometimes *vehemently* dislike them. In early 2004, for example, right around the time when Brandt was devising his "play to a standard" philosophy, a parent of a current player excoriated him for being too controlling, overbearing, inconsiderate, arrogant, and overall, for not letting the boys be regular college students. This parent's mushroom cloud of criticism scorched the coach for a full 40 minutes as Brandt, in his words, "just sat there and took it," legal pad in hand, chronicling the complaints. In the moment, Brandt's response was impassive: "I hear you and I'll consider some of the things you're saying."

He did consider them, relying on McCarty for counsel over the next couple days and contemplating how the team, who had just been bounced in PKs in the NCAA round of 32, might *never* make it back to the finals. Was he really becoming too dictatorial? Too insistent? An obstacle to success? Did he really need to back off on his demands?

Ultimately, Brandt concluded that he should do exactly the opposite. Some of his athletes were becoming insubordinate, defying the rules, and engaging in various forms of unhealthy weekend behavior. Cliques were emerging. Like this dad, some guys wanted the program to be run on their terms and it was threatening the culture.

So Brandt sat them down—the entire team at midnight after an indoor training session in January—and, as he tells it, "I let those guys have it. I just came out in the open and said I know what some of you guys are doing, I know there are different agendas, I know there's self-interest. And right there *I reset the course* for who we were. Purpose. Identity. I risked a mass exodus, but ... people were looking for compromise, so we made a stand. It was a key moment."

For sure. In the end, a few of the problem guys walked, the vast majority of the team stayed, redoubling their commitment, and Messiah got back on track.

That's another understatement, perhaps. Since that day, the Messiah men have won every national title, save one. Six of the last seven.

If "play to a standard" means anything, it means that the leader will be raising the bar—permanently—insisting on maximum effort, calling out non-adherents, quashing mediocrity, and unswervingly enforcing new thresholds of behavior. Periodically, it means to fearlessly "reset the course" to combat drift.

You've got two choices when confronting a challenge: shrink away from it or fight. I want you to fight.

From the men's summer training materials regarding the five minute mile

Asserting this kind of control is a pathway to lasting success, as we've seen, but make no mistake: It's by no means the Dale Carnegie pathway to "win friends and influence people"—at least not in the short run. Initially, you're more likely to lose friends and infuriate people.

But this is of no concern to the best coaches, the best executives, the best teachers and parents and pastors and politicians. They refuse to let the critics dictate the terms or the targets of their leadership.

The best musicians seem to operate this way, too. To quote U2's Bono, "Sing the melody line you hear in your own head. Remember, you don't owe anybody any explanations."

Now admittedly, if applied with complete abandon, that sort of advice might be problematic for anyone with a boss or a spouse or a cop in the rearview mirror. But it works well for singing and soccer. Aspire to something bigger than what everyone else considers success. Do it without "explanations," excuses or exceptions.

In this respect, Bono and Brandt are clearly kindred spirits. They encourage their teams and themselves to strive for perfection, to doggedly pursue excellence, to "play" to a standard all the time. They sustain success by killing complacency. They continue to hear the melody rather than the naysayers. They choose courage over capitulation.

This is what gets you to the big stage or the Big Dance. This is what keeps you there year after year. And this is what's made these guys award-winning leaders.

Some Other Enabling Conditions of Success

No U.S. college soccer program at any level had ever won the men's and women's championship in the same year. Messiah almost swept it in 2002, but the women came up just a goal short in the finals. Now, in 2005, both teams were back.

The women that year had survived a cardiac-kid playoff run that included a quarter-final win in PKs and an overtime victory in the semis. Into the championship they took an undefeated record—a record that would, in fact, remain that way at the final whistle. The game's only goal came off an acrobatic 35-yard handspring throw from Rachel Horning in the 70th minute, nodded in at the six by Billie Jo Adkins. "I've been doing that throw since I was nine years old," said Horning after the game. "If I just started to try the somersault now, I'd probably break my neck!"

Instead, it broke the back of a spirited College of New Jersey squad who, despite having a pacey All-American up top, couldn't manage an equalizer. Messiah's freshman sensation, Kacie Klynstra, won that battle all day, not even allowing a shot—a performance that earned Kacie the tournament's most outstanding player award.

Finally, in Frey's sixth season and the program's eighteenth, the Messiah women lifted the D3 trophy.

A few hours later, in a near carbon-copy match, the men's team also entered the final with an unblemished record, also scored late—in the 69th minute—and also emerged with a one-nil victory. Ryan Edwards got the game-winner, converting a Bryan Mohney feed and capping the men's second straight title, their fourth in six years.

December 2005. Messiah soccer had accomplished the unprecedented: Two national champions in the same year. The combined record of the teams was its own monument, an indomitable 46-0-1.

Hundreds upon hundreds of Messiah students were on hand to witness the event, an impressive turnout since that year the finals were held in Greensboro, North Carolina—over Thanksgiving weekend nonetheless. But the legions of faithful cut short their break and made the 400-mile trek down Interstate 81 for the Friday-Saturday contests.

"There was a good percentage of the student body there," star forward Annie Futato told the media. "They always support us at home and at our regular away games, but it was a long trip down after Thanksgiving."[26]

Support indeed. Over the years, attendance at the women's games has grown from a "good percentage of the student body" to a great percentage—figures that put them on the national map. In fact, in the 2010 season, attendance was 756 per home game, more than double the next closest D3 program, more than any D2 school, and, phenomenally for a college with an enrollment of 2,800, 34th in the country.[27]

The support at the men's games has also been historic. During seven seasons from 2000 to 2010, Messiah led all D3 schools in attendance. And remarkably, their 2010 average attendance of 1,709 not only put them ahead of all D3 and D2 schools, but at 14th in the nation, right between Penn

State and UNC, schools enrolling 43,000 and 29,000, respectively, at their main campuses.[28]

Is it any wonder that when *US News & World Report* recently published its "Top Colleges for Soccer Fans," the magazine ranked Messiah as third in the nation, behind only Indiana and UVA? It's a pretty remarkable place for those being cheered by these fans as well.[29]

A Supportive Environment

Beyond the seven disciplines described at in this book, there are some other conditions that enable Messiah soccer's success. Among them is the environment in which they play. Where can a college player go, even in Division I, and play in front of these kinds of crowds?

But the environmental influence is much bigger than this "twelfth man advantage" during games. Messiah is decidedly a soccer school. There's no competition with an American football team on this campus (Messiah simply doesn't have one), one sees soccer jerseys everywhere (not just Messiah jerseys, but Premier League, MLS, and others), and there's just a general buzz around campus on game days about whom they're playing and what's at stake.

The athletes feel important. And relevant, according to Scott Frey: "This place is about soccer. Players and coaches feel that what we do matters to people."

But does the soccer culture matter when it comes to soccer results?

It may if the academic studies are to be believed. A long line of research points to the "external support and recognition" of the larger organization as one of the major contributors of team effectiveness. "External support," in these studies, is not primarily financial resources (in fact, according to one program insider, the budget throughout the Brandt years was "laughable" and did not increase from 2001 to 2008, despite all those championships.) Rather, it's an overall culture of affirmation that can sometimes influence motivation, commitment, and even the success of a team.[30]

Indiana University,
The University of Virginia,
Messiah College

The top three colleges in the nation for soccer fans, according to *US News & World Report*, 2010

The affirmation has clearly been there throughout from the student body. It's also been emerging over the decades from the Administration. Long-time Coach Layton Shoemaker recalls: "(Former President) Ray Hostetter was really supportive. Messiah was a sleepy college, not well recognized, but he and other campus leaders saw athletics as a way to grow the reputation and recognition."

Slowly, he says, the Administration began turning a corner on the issue in meaningful ways. For example, back in the day, Shoemaker was swamped with other responsibilities. He was not only the men's coach for 23 years, but also the chairman of the "Health, Physical Education, and Recreation" Department for 17 of those years, Athletic Director for 15, and teaching classes for all 23. "I couldn't devote as much attention to soccer as I should have," he offers candidly.

But over time, the College increasingly permitted coaches to be coaches. They are indeed tasked with some other duties, including occasional teaching, but on balance, says Frey, "I think we have a good Administration that allows us to do what we need to do and gives us what we need to do it."

That kind of structure, more typical of D1 than D3 schools, provides space for the critical but time-consuming approaches like "both-and" recruiting, cultivating team chemistry, and creating customized practices—staples of Messiah's competitive advantage—to become a reality. Says Shoemaker, reflecting on how to take a program to the next level of excellence: "When you're trying to do something special in an environment like we have at Messiah (i.e., no scholarships and academics first), the people above you have to buy in."

Increasingly, they have in important ways. College administrators show up for home games as well as Final Fours. Faculty members regularly chat with the players about the games' special moments and the upcoming schedule. And the College President even invites the teams to her house for post-season celebrations. Says former captain J.D. Binger, "President Phipps makes you feel so valued. She's outstanding. The team invitations to her home, the congratulatory emails … It's the little things that make a really big difference."[31]

Hiring from Within

At present, Messiah soccer employs four coaches for the women's team and four for the men's team. Every one of them played his or her college soccer at Messiah. Many of the former coaches were once Messiah players as well.

It's not convenience, it's strategic. And it may be another enabling condition of success.

By hiring from within, Messiah keeps its essential core values in place. There's continuity to its purposes and its processes since the entire leadership team has lived them from the inside. Beyond that, these are committed, compassionate people who care about the program and the players and whose enthusiasm is contagious. "There is just a love that assistant coaches have for Messiah soccer," Women's Assistant Coach Bethany (Swanger) Sauer says with a smile, "and the players catch it!"

There is just a love that assistant coaches have for Messiah soccer and the players catch it.

Bethany (Swanger) Sauer
Class of 2003, Women's Assistant Coach

Moreover, the people they hire have the soccer acumen and communication skills to be credible and to make great players even greater. Most were standouts themselves, some even All-Americans. Every one of them could be a head coach somewhere else, if they chose to be. And those who are head coaches at Messiah could be coaching in D1 for a lot more money.

Brad McCarty explains why they don't: "Some of this has to do with a desire to give back to an institution that has done so much for you. People are willing to take less money to be part of (this) environment."[32]

They stay in the environment a long time, too. For example, Shoemaker was in the head coaching role for 23 years. Brandt was a Messiah assistant and head coach for 21 years. Frey's tenure in Messiah leadership spans 17 years. McCarty is currently in his eleventh year on the Falcon sideline.

Getting the right people on the bus at Messiah clearly applies to more than the players. They've tapped leaders who were on the bus already, who thoroughly understand how it works, and who have for years been able to turbo-charge the thing.

A Coaching Style that Fits the Situation

But when it comes to head coaches at Messiah, it's not enough to just select an insider or someone with a soccer IQ of 200. Messiah has bounded from good to great to unique during the past decade because these guys also have a coaching style that fits the situation.

It wouldn't be a controversial statement to say that Brandt, Frey and McCarty are essentially "benevolent dictators." That's their basic leadership persona. This is not a democracy and their word is ultimately law. At the same time, they genuinely love the men and women God has entrusted to them and they have a burning desire to disciple them—benevolently.

However, the personality similarities come to a screeching halt after that, as each of the coaches will tell you.

Dave Brandt can seem like an army drill sergeant (despite his current position at Navy). Insistent and even intimidating, if you don't comply it's drop and give me twenty—or maybe twenty thousand. Not literally, of course, but Coach Brandt is clearly in charge, he has clear standards, and at practice, he's heard clearly across campus. His intensity can be daunting to some players, especially at first, as is his zero tolerance policy for mediocrity. At the same time, Brandt cares deeply about his boys and works hard to develop healthy relationships. In his words, as we first heard back in Discipline 2, "I will always go and do something about it if I feel the relationship is in jeopardy at any moment." Highly demanding but highly relational. It's the kind of "both-and" approach he champions in every other area of the program.

Scott Frey, by contrast, is an easy going guy who, at the same time, is exceedingly driven. Frey is your classic "Level 5 Leader" in the Jim Collins sense, personifying both great humility and at the same time great zeal. His gregarious persona belies the gritty determination that has pushed this program upwards since his appointment. Players and alums simply rave about the man, with not one of my many interviewees offering a hint of criticism.

Brad McCarty is different still, more of a free spirit. He was a bit of a rebel in college, at least from a Messiah perspective, a bit of a joker, and as Brandt's assistant, provided the guys with some welcome comic relief. At the same time, McCarty is as competitive as they come and extremely comfortable with candor, calling out the guys as quickly as Brandt did. "That's a strength of mine," says the current Coach. "I have no problem addressing issues head-on."

Well, so what? People are different. Why does any of this matter? Simply because the personalities and leadership styles of these three men have perfectly fit the situational and gender differences on their teams.

For example, Brandt took over a team in 1997 that probably needed a single-minded autocrat if it was to break free of its cultural inertia. Good was no longer going to be good enough. Soccer could no longer be just another activity for these students. And guys, no matter how talented they were, could no longer choose to do things their own way. The kind of realignment that nineteen-year-old boys need to become an elite team necessitated Brandt-style leadership.

But by the time McCarty took over the program in 2009, the culture and systems were firmly in place (he had, of course, helped create them) and Messiah now needed someone with the wisdom and humility to sustain the success, rather than someone who would insist on putting his own stamp on the program. As McCarty tells it: "Ninety-five percent of the program is the same and five percent is different. That five percent is personality. I'm more willing to delegate." Consequently, two years into his head coaching gig, McCarty has earned two more NCAA rings. It seems he was the right man at the right time.

Male and female athletes are motivated by different things and coaches need to be sensitive to this.

Todd Balsbaugh
Class of 1994, Women's Assistant Coach

Consider Scott Frey as well. When he stepped into the women's coaching role in 2000, Frey inherited a more compliant culture than Brandt had, though one that also required some realigning and innovation if it was to break through. As such, his personality blend of grace with zeal—a mirror image of so many of his players—was exactly right. When one is leading the willing, similarity is the right fit. Beyond that, coaching women requires different sensitivities, not the least of which is that *the coach has to build relationships based on the women as people rather than as players*. Not everyone has disposition to do that.

Few understand this dynamic better than UNC women's coach Anson Dorrance, seven time national coach of the year and twenty time national champion. He writes, in his popular book *Training Soccer Champions*:

> "(We are) trying to set up a team community. It's a community of people of equal value, which is almost a contradiction in athletics. But I think you can create this community if the players understand that you respect them based on things beyond their athletic performance. With a women's team, it's critical to establish this because they are too mature to feel that athletics has any superior value.
>
> "Those of us who come from men's athletics seem to feel that sports do have something intrinsically valuable. Women think that's absurd..."

So in light of the difference, the point for coaches, according to Dorrance, is this:

> "Building (women's) confidence through athletics is a direct demonstration that you are concerned with them as people first and as competitors second. If your connection is based on the athletic hierarchy, you're not going to create community, you're not going to gain the respect of the reserve players and you're not going to create positive team chemistry."[33]

Although Brandt and McCarty aspire to do the same with their guys—to relate to them as people first and players second—Frey is a master at this. It's simply who he is, so it flows quite naturally. As much as he's benchmarked the Messiah men's system and reapplied it to his own, player relationships is one area where he has brilliantly leveraged his own innate gifts to build an outstanding community. For over a decade, he's been a coach of grace creating a "team of grace."

The point of all this is that leadership style really does matter, but there's not one ideal type. Rather, a reason Messiah has enjoyed so much success since the late 1990's is because *they've hired leaders who fit the situation.* A turnaround or realignment requires something different from what it takes to sustain success. Leading women requires something different from what it takes to lead men.

A leadership style that fits. It's an intangible asset that only seems to get noticed when things go poorly. But at Messiah, it's an essential reason that things go well.

Coaches Who Are Credible

There's another enabling condition of success related to the coaches. Players follow them steadfastly. They reliably do what the coaches tell them to do. They trust them. It's every leader's ideal.

The reason goes beyond the fact that the coaches are smart or have an impressive player resume or that they're likable people. It goes beyond the fact that there are consequences of not following. More fundamentally, players closely follow the coaches' instructions because the coaches are credible.

Not just persuasive or inspiring or intelligent, but *credible.* Their results prove that they can get the job done. And according to some of the best social science research available, it's arguably the most important characteristic for any leader. For example, James Kouzes and Barry Posner, probably the most cited leadership researchers on the planet, summarize it well: "If people don't believe in the messenger, they won't believe in the message. If they don't believe in you, they won't believe in what you say."[34]

Coach Frey doesn't have that problem. "If I tell them I think it'll work, then they think it'll work," he says, adding that this is a blessing he does not take for granted. "If we would do all these things and we weren't successful, however we might define that, then they're looking at me saying 'why should I listen to you?' Now I feel like I could ask them to do anything and they say okay because there's a trust, a belief, a confidence that comes from past results."

Brandt, too, made this point, in the context of his intense practices. "Why work so hard at this?" he asks rhetorically. "Because every minute of practice matters and I've been able to convince my teams of that. They know it matters. But you've got to back that up with results. College kids aren't stupid and they're not going to be fooled."

The coaches' pragmatism puts them in good company. It was no less an intellect than Peter Drucker who famously said "Effective leadership is not about making speeches or being liked. Leadership is defined by results, not attributes." When you get results—when you're credible—people trust your judgment. People seek your perspective. People follow, often generating even better results. It's the essence of leadership

But you can't demand it. It doesn't come with the title or the degrees. You earn it over time. That's an important caveat.

Here's another, but a more liberating one: Earning credibility doesn't require winning a national championship. Even small results, as long as they're meaningful to the team, will give you traction. A new recruiting strategy that lands a special player. A new formation that repeatedly pays dividends. A drill that clearly makes a difference in a match. A better record this year than last year, which was better than the year before that.

"How does it happen?" asks Frey, answer readily at hand. "Little steps. Little successes. Success gives you credibility."

Confidence through Winning

Winning yields another benefit beyond building the coaches' credibility, a benefit that tends to culminate in even more victories. That benefit is confidence.

In countless human endeavors, from public speaking to test-taking to athletic competition, confidence is a psychological driver of performance. Our personal experience bears witness to this. So does an abundance of research on "team efficacy": What a team believes about its capabilities affects how it performs. Success can breed success; failure can breed failure.

It's not automatic, of course, but it seems to have made a real difference for the Messiah teams—in particular, when it's mattered the most.

Current Men's Assistant Aaron Faro explains: "We now have the collective belief that we can win no matter what. That's especially helpful when we're down a goal or two—the collective belief remains and we find a way to come back. We won in overtime six times in 2010, including the National Championship, in part because of that confidence and experience of being down and coming back."

"Run at them, press them, and when they get tired, run at them!" As I heard Coach say this, I looked around the room at the faces of my teammates. I was never more confident that we were going to win the last game of the season.

Amy Horst
Class of 2010

Faro also knows this from his time between the lines, having been an integral part of the breakthrough teams that secured the program's first national titles. Referring to that era, former player and long-time program observer Tim Houseal makes the point succinctly: "After the 2000 championship, we knew. You do it once you can do it again. We went from being a top ten program perennially to being the top program in the country. Part of that change was winning our first national championship."

I went to the source with this one, Dave Brandt. As a player and coach, he had spent nineteen seasons with Messiah teams that almost made it to the top and then, the inflection point—six of his next nine seasons they won it all. How critical is the confidence and commitment that comes from winning?

Brandt answered it in his current context as the head coach of Navy, a program that was struggling when he took over in 2009. "Winning fuels belief," he began, "It fuels buy-in, and you hate to say that, but ... if we can just get a few breaks and win a few critical games next year, it's going to explode. If we don't, it's not going to implode and there's nothing inherently different. We're still doing good things ... but I could really use the winning piece."

It's another catalyst of success. Winning creates confidence. Confidence enables our best effort, which in turn creates more winning. It becomes a virtuous cycle, spiraling upward toward a new day.

Epilogue

Beyond Doubt

Dave Brandt likes to share this story with coaches and other leaders as a reminder of what they're up against. It's more than some stiff competition.

In spring 1997, soon after he was promoted to the position of Head Coach, he ran into a Messiah faculty member who, he says, "probably just to be nice and polite, asked me 'What are the big plans?'"

To the best of his recollection, effervescing with ideas and idealism, he "talked for about a minute straight, which is a long time in a setting like that when she's essentially asking 'how are you and I hope things go well.' And though I don't remember exactly what I said, I basically described what I would call 'Camelot on the soccer field.' I told her 'this is *really* going to be something else. We are going to have *unbelievable* guys in the program. We are going to achieve, guys are going to get along, we're going to make the whole greater than the sum of the parts, this is going to be an *awesome* experience and, besides all that, we're going to win national championships."

With a wry grin Brandt completes the story: "I'll never forget her reaction. She smiled, she looked at me, she shook her head and said, 'oh ... you're young'—as if to pat me on the head and say 'well, that's nice to have those dreams, but you'll eventually find out like the rest of us that things don't always work out and you might have to settle for just whatever you get.'"[35]

He painted an idealistic vision of the future. Understandably, perhaps, she doubted.

Fortunately, Brandt did not. He forged ahead, flanked by Jason Spodnik and eventually Scott Frey and Brad McCarty. Gradually, and intrepidly, they built a new era.

He who aims for nothing is sure to hit it.

Layton Shoemaker
Men's Head Coach, 1974-1996

When a leader pursues great change, as we said in Discipline 7, that leader will encounter great opposition. In the same way, he or she will also encounter great doubt. It can be every bit as inhibiting.

Often that doubt comes from others, either overtly or subtly, but just as often it comes from oneself. We ask, privately and painfully, "Who am I to make these bold moves? What if this doesn't work? Am I even allowed to think this way? What if others knew just how unsure of myself I am? And why should anyone follow *me*?"

Self-doubt can be more debilitating than the misgivings of others. We can escape others' comments, but we can't seem to escape our toxic self-talk. The doubts proliferate, one giving license to the next. Eventually, we choose to play it safe, deferring the dream, and sadly, next year becomes the same as this one.

That's not leadership. It's the dictatorship of doubt. And it's so pervasive that psychologists actually have named it: "the impostor syndrome." Many high achievers are actually convinced deep down that they're frauds, dismissing earlier accomplishments as luck or timing. It can be absolutely paralyzing if we let it be, quashing our potential and that of our teams. We're left hoping for something better, but unwilling to take the necessary risks to get there.

It doesn't have to be that way. Every coach and every leader can get beyond it—beyond doubt.

The Messiah coaches, you might be surprised to learn, are a living testimony to that. Scott Frey, for example, admits to some real trepidation when he stepped into his first head coaching job at Alma College. "I vividly remember thinking a few days before my first pre-season practice, 'what am I going to bring to these guys that will cause them to believe in me and trust that I know what I am doing?' These weren't boys, these were young men and I wasn't much older than they were. I had no resume of success, nothing to hang my hat on as to why they should believe in me."

But he persevered through the doubts and within a few years had brought Alma men's team all the way to the Final Four.

In the same way, Brad McCarty asks, still a bit daunted by succeeding a legend, "What kind of fool follows a guy who wins six championships in nine years?" He remembers being offered the top job, reflecting on the emotional energy and mental effort that Brandt expended and wondering: "can *I* really do that?"

But he took the job anyway, setting aside his doubts, and kept the championship streak alive.

And it's not just on the front end of the job that doubts creep in. Even with his name atop all these lists of successful coaches, Dave Brandt admits to still being "confident but scared to death at the same time. As sure of myself as I am, I'm not sure of myself."

But he presses on, heavily leaning on others as sounding boards, learning continuously, reinventing ideas and recommitting to lead beyond himself.

Despite their uncertainties, these men forged ahead, sometimes making radical changes, they worked indefatigably, and in the end, they reaped stunning success measured both in victories and in changed lives, their higher purpose. They overcame their doubts, overcame their fears, and overcame their skeptics to achieve breakthrough success. They're proof of the possible.

This is a pivotal lesson that they learned, at least in part, from their common mentor. For years, one of Layton Shoemaker's stock phrases was: "He who aims for nothing is sure to hit it." It's a message that transcended his career: We don't have to aim aimlessly. We don't have to be a slave to doubt or to the status quo. We don't have to just hope for better results, no matter what our present team looks like. Instead, those who are serious about excellence can adopt a road-tested model for how excellence happens—one that has elevated a college soccer program to an unprecedented level of success this past decade.

"The model," says Dave Brandt in summary, "is not soccer-specific and I don't even think it's necessarily sports-specific. I would call it a model for creating a championship culture among any group of people—something that any leader could glean something from."

It's worth considering, without a doubt. The Messiah Method may indeed work in places other than Messiah College.

Notes

1. Erik Brady, "At Messiah, glory comes on, off field," *USA Today*, October 20, 2009, C1.

2. "David H. Brandt," *Beyond the Bottom Line* (Messiah College Department of Management & Business), Summer 2005, p. 6

3. Rebecca Jekel, "At the top of their games," *The Bridge* (Messiah College), Winter 2006, p. 16.

4. Jeremy Elliott, "Final Four X 2," *The Patriot-News*, November 24, 2005, 12-13

5. Corey Furman, 2009, "Getting to the bottom of absurdity," http://www.messiah.edu/athletics/articles/furm/12809-itnevergetsold.html

6. Layton Shoemaker, "Sportsmanship: Playing for Higher Stakes," *The Bridge*(Messiah College), April 1989, 8-10

7. John Wooden and Steve Jamison, *Wooden on Leadership*, McGraw Hill 2005, p. xi and p. 42

8. Gary Emmons, 2007, "When good teams go bad," *HBS Working Knowledge*, http://hbswk.hbs.edu/item/5602.html

9. Erik Brady, "At Messiah, glory comes on, off field," *USA Today*, October 20, 2009, C1.

10. "Blossey's hero act propels Messiah to national championship," 2008, www.messiah.edu/athletics/sports/mens_soccer/articles/0809/dec-6.html

11. John Kotter, *Leading Change,* Harvard Business Press: Cambridge MA, 1996.

12. From personal conversations and from Peggy Koach, 2011, "Messiah student-athlete lends discouraged professor a key assist," http://storylink.messiah.edu/?p=910

13. Any Farnum, "Messiah men, women still perfect," *The Sentinel,* November 11, 2005, C1.

14. Rebecca Jekel, "At the top of their games," *The Bridge*(Messiah College), Winter 2006, p. 16.

15. Jeremy Elliott, "Final Four X 2," *The Patriot-News*, November 24, 2005, 12-13

16. From www.messiah.edu/athletics/sports/womens_soccer/pages/recruiting-form.html

17. Any Farnum, "Messiah men, women still perfect," *The Sentinel,* November 11, 2005, C1.

18. Michael Klausner and David Hoch, "Creating Team Chemistry," *Soccer Journal*, 1997, www.nscaa.com/subpages/20060331162209107.php

19. "David H. Brandt," *Beyond the Bottom Line*(Messiah College Department of Management & Business), Summer 2005, p. 6

20. Alex Ferguson with Hugh McIlvanney, *Managing My Life: My Autobiography*, (Coronet Books: London), 2000, p. 219.

21. Thanks to team manager Randy Herndon (and his manuscript, *Perspectives from the Tent,* 2003) for this insight, as well as for some other information used in this section.

22. Rebecca Jekel, "At the top of their games," *The Bridge* (Messiah College),Winter 2006, p. 16.

23. Phil Soto-Ortiz, "'Playing for something more,'" *The Patriot News*, December 12, 2010, F21-23.

24. Alex Ferguson with Hugh McIlvanney, *Managing My Life: My Autobiography*, (Coronet Books: London), 2000, p. 137.

25. Daniel F. Chambliss (1989), "The Mundanity of Excellence: An Ethnographic Report on Stratification and Olympic Swimmers," *Sociological Theory* 7 (1):70-86.

26. Toni Fitzgerald, "Messiah Relished 'Title Town' Status," *The Sentinel*, December 4, 2005, A1, A4

27. From "Women's Soccer Attendance Records," 2010, http://fs.ncaa.org/Docs/stats/w_soccer_RB/2011/attend.pdf

28. From "Men's Attendance Records," 2010, http://fs.ncaa.org/Docs/stats/ m_soccer_RB/2011/attend.pdf

29. From “9 top colleges for soccer fans,” www.usnews.com/education/slideshows/9-of-the-best-colleges-for-soccer-fans/3

30. For summaries of this research, see, Carl Larson and Frank Lafasto, *Teamwork: What Must Go Right, What Can Go Wrong* (1989), especially chapter 8, and J. Richard Hackman, *Leading Teams: Setting the Stage for Great Performances*, (2002), especially chapter 5.

31. Cory Furman, 2009, “The blind date that *had* to happen,” www.messiah.edu/athletics/articles/furm/21709-soccerlove.html

32. Phil Soto-Ortiz, “‘Playing for something more,’” *The Patriot News*, December 12, 2010, F21-23.

33. Anson Dorrance, *Training Soccer Champions*, JTC Sports, 1996, pp. 79-80

34. James Kouzes and Barry Posner *Credibility: How Leaders Gain and Lose It, Why People Demand It* (2003). See also their seminal work, *The Leadership Challenge* (1987, 2007).

35. Dave Brandt related this story in a DVD entitled “Building a Championship Culture” produced by Championship Productions in 2009.